YORK NOT[

General Editors: Professor A.N[
of Stirling) & Professor Suheil [
University of Beirut*)

CW00556976

Charles Dickens

DOMBEY AND SON

Notes by Suzanne Brown

BA (MOUNT HOLYOKE) PH D (DUBLIN)

LONGMAN
YORK PRESS

YORK PRESS
Immeuble Esseily, Place Riad Solh, Beirut.

LONGMAN GROUP (UK) LTD
Longman House,
Burnt Mill,
Harlow,
Essex

First published 1986

ISBN 0-582-78299-6

Produced by Longman Group (FE) Ltd
Printed in Hong Kong

Contents

Part 1

Introduction

The life of Charles Dickens

Charles Dickens was born on 7 February 1812 in a pleasant terrace house in the seaport of Portsmouth. Five months later the Dickens family moved to a cheaper house, the start of a social migration from the middle classes to real poverty and back again. When he was two, the family went to live in London. They stayed there for nearly three years until they entered a period of relative prosperity in which they lived in Chatham, then a busy seaport thirty miles from London. Charles and the other children were often minded by two kindly servants, Jane Bonny and Mary Weller, whose wild tales kindled sparks in Charles's own overheated imagination.

In his boyhood Charles loved exuberant melodrama and singing. He had a hectic zest for life, tempered by secret childish fears. His father would often allow him and his sister Fanny to entertain a crowd at the Mitre Inn by standing on a table, and singing sea duets. The variety, the colour, the sheer physical presence of so much life, and so many objects, crowded in on young Dickens till the world seemed a place imagination could scarcely describe, let alone control. He and his brother Fred used to mimic nautical conversations, or put on impromptu magic lantern shows in the family kitchen.

He loved reading; his favourite stories came from the *Arabian Nights* and a fairy tale collection called *Mother Bunch*. He enjoyed eighteenth century novels such as Henry Fielding's *Tom Jones* (1749) Tobias Smollett's *Roderick Random* (1748) and Laurence Sterne's *Tristam Shandy* (1759). As he grew old enough for visits to the theatre he discovered the greatness of clowns, and the magic of pantomime. He loved to mock makeshift Shakespearean productions, and enthusiastically joined a distant relative just down from Sandhurst in going to the Theatre Royal.

Although Charles Dickens had many reservations about his parents, he often enjoyed their company. His mother awakened his love of reading, and he certainly shared his father's pleasure in long chatty walks. But happy memories of such activities co-existed in Dickens's mind with bitter perceptions of the inadequate provision his parents made for their children. John Dickens could not stay out of debt and was arrested and put in the Marshalsea Debtors Prison when Charles was twelve. Most of the family lived with him in prison, but Fanny went to the Royal Academy of Music, and Charles worked in a factory labelling boot-blacking bottles. He hated this time of his life with an abiding passion; it marked his caricaturing imagination. Long London walks in the months before a legacy enabled John Dickens to leave prison made Charles a street-wanderer who reacted deeply to all he saw.

Dickens's family lived a life of perpetual hope doomed to disappointment. Charles's father sent him to Wellington Academy, and, at fifteen, Charles was able to become a legal clerk. He determined to rise socially by his own efforts. He studied shorthand and became a freelance reporter of Doctors' Commons cases and later of parliamentary proceedings. He wrote first for his uncle's paper, *Mirror of Parliament*, and later also for an evening paper, *The True Sun*. Then he was offered a post on the *Morning Chronicle*. He began to publish literary sketches, first anonymously, and then under the pen-name of Boz. His first book, *Sketches by Boz*, illustrated by George Cruikshank, was published in February 1836. Dickens was then twenty-four and just finding his way. *Pickwick Papers*, begun later that year, convinced him that he was a writer and he left newspaper reporting behind. The success of *Pickwick Papers* surpassed Dickens's wildest dreams. Having by this time married Catherine Hogarth, he was greatly relieved to find himself financially prosperous. Catherine's sister Mary and Charles's brother Fred both lived with the young couple, and Dickens became very close to Mary. Her sudden death in May 1837 overcame him with sorrow. It haunted him, but created in his imagination the figure of a gentle woman untouched by worldliness. Rose Maylie in *Oliver Twist* and Agnes Wickfield in *David Copperfield* are characters of this kind. Florence Dombey is more complex, although she too undergoes suffering without losing her essential sweetness.

Dickens's marriage was not happy. He still resented having been turned down by Maria Beadnell, a banker's daughter, and he missed Mary a great deal, continuing to mourn for her. His wife could not offer him intellectual companionship as the family grew, and Dickens was restless and touchy. After twenty-two years they separated and Dickens's household was run by his sister-in-law Georgina Hogarth. Perhaps this is why the older women characters in Dickens's stories are often good-hearted spinsiters. Throughout his life Dickens sought to describe the happy home which he created in his mind out of a child's longing for harmony and peace. The dark alienation of unhappy family life is something he explores with dignity and sympathetic understanding in *Dombey and Son*.

By 1837 Dickens was editing a magazine for the publisher Bentley, and writing monthly instalments of both *Pickwick Papers* and *Oliver*

Twist. Before *Oliver Twist* was finished he was already writing *Nicholas Nickleby*. In 1839 he began a new weekly magazine, *Master Humphrey's Clock*, to which he contributed weekly instalments of *The Old Curiosity Shop*, a very popular novel about a child's suffering and death, which had something of the quality of a fairy tale. It was followed by *Barnaby Rudge* (1841), a story set in the not very distant past of the Gordon Riots of 1780. The magazine ended with the conclusion of *Barnaby Rudge*, but in 1850 Dickens began a new weekly journal, *Household Words*. This covered all topics from a rag fair in Paris to Mr Ball's somnambulist. The magazine and its successor (from 1859), *All the Year Round*, gave Dickens the direct relationship with his public that he obviously needed. It also contained instalments of novels by Dickens and others. Dickens never stopped writing in this difficult and demanding form: he saw himself as an entertainer, a role he never despised, and writing in instalments kept him in touch with his readers' responses. As part of this relationship he wrote a series of Christmas books. The first, *A Christmas Carol*, was a great success. It was followed by *The Chimes* (1844), *The Cricket on the Hearth* (1845), *The Battle of Life* (1846) and *The Haunted Man* (1848).

Martin Chuzzlewit began to appear in January 1842, and Dickens worked steadily at it despite travelling to America for six months of that year. He was torn between a longing for affection and tranquillity, and a deep, restless hunger for new sights and new places. He travelled to Italy with his family in 1844, but returned home to read *The Chimes* aloud to a circle of friends. In 1846 he published *Pictures From Italy*, which was something in the nature of a travelogue. Dickens's mixed feelings about the past had been intensified by travel, and later in *Household Words* (1851, 1852, 1853) he published *A Child's History of England*.

He soon felt the need to travel again. In 1846, while beginning *Dombey and Son*, he went to Switzerland, and then to Paris. He was to return to Paris several times during the 1850s. Despite these travels his feelings about contemporary England are vivid in *Dombey and Son*. The railway, which so radically changed English life, brings prosperity to the humble neighbourhood of the Toodles, but is also a symbol of energy and death. Sol Gills's shop, despite selling scientific instruments, is out of touch with the pace of nineteenth-century life, and someone of simple heart and independent means, such as Mr Toots, cannot find his niche. A great house such as Dombey's can fall mysteriously. Nineteenth-century England seems to project ruthless challenge and change.

Dickens's next book was *David Copperfield* (1849–50), the most autobiographical of his novels. It concentrates more on particular people's lives and conveys less sense of social pressures. But he returned to social themes with *Bleak House* (1852–3) and *Hard Times* (1854). *Little Dorrit* (1855–7) was also an attack on social injustices, tracing in them the old pattern of human indifference struggling with individual human caring.

A Tale of Two Cities (1859), however, is again more a direct story than a heavily symbolic work, perhaps because it describes France more than the England Dickens knew so well. *Great Expectations* (1860–1) and *Our Mutual Friend* (1864–5) have an almost fairy-tale quality about their atmosphere, and a view of the world which is child-like in its wonder and passivity. Dickens's good characters often find solace and redemption in their relations with other people. But the world around them is such that only a few can find their place in it, and many remain in misery. Dickens's last novel, *The Murder of Edwin Drood*, is a dark and ominous book, and is unfinished.

Charles Dickens was an obsessive worker, and poured energy into being a literary man, a theatre-goer, and a good provider both for his growing family and for his needy relations. He knew many people but perhaps his close friendship with John Forster was one of the few relationships in which he allowed himself to receive help, rather than to master others by his magnetism. Forster sorted out Dickens's difficulties with publishers, calmed him down when he was worried about his writing, and, late in life, wrote the first biography of his friend. When Dickens died on 8 June 1870, he left behind a circle of close friends, a large and restless family, and a memory of his own vitality so intense that it makes his death seem almost impossible and absurd.

A note on the text

Dombey and Son first appeared in pamphlets of thirty-two pages between October 1846 and April 1848, and was highly successful. Charles Dickens himself checked the 1867 edition from which many modern editions take their texts. The fullest edition of Dickens's complete works is *The Centenary Edition of the Works of Charles Dickens*, Chapman and Hall, London; Charles Scribner's Sons, New York, 1911. A complete edition currently in print is *The New Oxford Illustrated Dickens*, Oxford University Press, London, 1948– .

Part 2

Summaries

of DOMBEY AND SON

A general summary

Dombey and Son tells the story of the Dombey household over the period of years in which Dombey's loving daughter grows up. In the opening chapter Mrs Dombey dies, giving birth to Paul. A kindly nurse, Polly Toodle, is hired, and she comforts young Florence as well as caring for Paul. Florence has a staunch friend in her maid Susan Nipper, and so the three form a sort of family away from Dombey's scrutiny. The three secretly decide to visit Polly's own family. On that fateful day Florence becomes lost and is first harassed and later abandoned by an old woman, Mrs Brown. She is rescued and brought to his friends at The Wooden Midshipman (a shop selling nautical instruments) by young Walter Gay, who has just begun work in her father's house of business. Dombey resents this, as he resents any help given by his social inferiors. In a rage, he dismisses Polly.

Eventually Paul and Florence are sent to school in Brighton. Paul is proving serious and solemn, an old child whose frailty touches the hearts of everyone. He first studies with Florence at Mrs Pipchin's and later, alone, at Dr Blimper's academy, where Florence secretly helps him with the excessive work. But his health is fragile, and he dies.

Florence takes this blow as well as she can. She cannot share the burden with her father, who mainly feels the loss of the continuation of the family business, and who has no wish to share his grief with her. She is a young girl now, and lives quietly with Susan in a couple of rooms of the big house. Mr Toots, a schoolfellow of Paul's, calls on her and gives her Diogenes, a huge friendly dog who will guard and comfort her. She also continues to visit the people at The Wooden Midshipman.

Mr Dombey has a jealous confidential clerk, Mr Carker, whose malevolence is general and extends even to young Walter. Carker persuades Dombey to send Walter to Barbados on the ship still named *Son and Heir*. After Paul's death Mr Dombey decides to go on holiday with a new acquaintance, Major Joe Bagstock. This convivial flatterer leads Dombey to propose marriage to Edith Granger, who will feel deeply that she is selling herself in alluring Dombey.

Their marriage is extremely unhappy. Edith, however, is greatly drawn to Florence, and mothers her as best she can. Carker notices all

this and tortures Edith by saying that her care of Florence will only em-
bitter Dombey against them both. Dombey cannot bear that Edith and,
earlier, Paul should have felt more for Florence than for himself.

Walter's boat is shipwrecked and his uncle Sol Gills disappears, leaving his friend Captain Cuttle to mind his shop and keep a home ready
for Walter. Florence and Susan share Captain Cuttle's terrible anxiety.
Mr Toots also visits Captain Cuttle and strikes up an unusual friendship. Polly Toodle's shifty son Rob works in The Wooden Midshipman as the Captain's helper, but in reality he is spying for Carker.
After a year, he leaves.

Suddenly the Captain's former landlady, Mrs MacStinger, turns up,
to frighten and berate Captain Cuttle. It is a year after Sol Gills's departure, so, in the presence of his friend Bunsby the Captain opens the
envelope containing his last will and a letter saying he is searching for
Walter. The Captain turns to Bunsby for help with Mrs MacStinger,
and Bunsby even persuades Mrs MacStinger to return the Captain's
trunk to him.

Meanwhile Carker presses Edith Dombey to run away with him, as a
revenge on Dombey. Edith has made a last plea to Dombey for mutual
tolerance, which fails, so in her despair her attitude to Carker weakens.

At this time, his brother and sister, John and Harriet Carker, make a
new friend, who wishes to remain unnoticed. He simply calls once a
week to see if all is well, and leaves immediately. Harriet also meets
Alice Brown, a woman who was transported to Australia after she had
been seduced by a man and had taken to crime. Harriet tries to help.
The reader watches Alice meet her own mother, who is the same Mrs
Brown who had once harassed Florence. The reader also learns that it
was James Carker who had ruined Alice.

Florence makes a journey to Brighton, secretly followed by Mr
Toots. They meet and share memories, and Mr Toots asks Florence if
she will consider marrying him. She turns him down gently.

Meanwhile Edith's mother, the worldly Mrs Skewton, dies slowly
after several strokes. Edith is with her, nursing her, and trying to
achieve some real contact with her. If this happens it is momentary and
sad. Dombey has an accident but chooses to recover at Mrs Pipchin's
rather than at home. Edith begins to feel real sorrow over their failing
marriage, and real love for Florence.

Then Susan Nipper confronts the ailing Dombey, attacking his neglect of Florence. She is dismissed. She meets Mr Toots, who helps her
to get a coach. He tells her she can only love Florence as much as he
does, not more.

Another disaster hits Florence. Edith does leave Dombey and when
Florence tries to comfort him he strikes her. She leaves home and goes to
The Wooden Midshipman, where Captain Cuttle takes her in.

One day, to their utter amazement, Walter returns. Mr Toots has been calling occasionally to see Captain Cuttle, and so he is able to tell Susan about Florence. She too comes to The Wooden Midshipman. The reunion is made complete when Sol Gills returns. He explains that he sent letters to Captain Cuttle at Mrs MacStinger's, but that lady never passed them on.

Walter asks Florence to marry him, and she agrees. Her new life begins as Edith's old life ends. Dombey pursues Edith and James Carker. Carker himself has been watched by Alice Brown as she vents her anger at him. She relents at the last minute, and tells Harriet that through her and her mother Dombey has learned where Carker has gone and is following him. Harriet tries to send a warning messenger.

Edith and Carker confront each other. She rebels against him and is defending herself with a knife when English voices are heard outside their French hotel room. Edith flees in one direction, Carker in another. He is pursued, and Dombey just comes close enough to see him plunge to his death under a roaring train.

Dombey lives on, but in financial ruin, which is only alleviated by money sent anonymously by Harriet and John Carker. Eventually he is reconciled with Florence and, through her, forgives Edith. Dombey lives to enjoy his grandchildren. Susan Nipper marries Mr Toots, and, in a generous gesture, Dickens unites Cornelia Blimper with one of Paul's tutors, Mr Feeder. Harriet Carker marries her quiet friend, Mr Morfin. The novel's ending is almost Shakespearian, with all these weddings taking place, but Dickens looks into the future and shows us Florence and Susan as happy mothers of several children.

This long and serious novel is a major work in its depth of psychological perception and its broad social vision. It is not a reformer's book because it is about private lives. Given the wickedness of some of the characters, it is a strangely compassionate book, but its very compassion makes it sad, as the reader is left with an impression of both the goodness and joy that have survived, and of happiness lost.

Detailed summaries

Chapter 1: Dombey and Son

Paul Dombey is born, and his mother dies. The older Dombey child, Florence, is left to act as Paul's mother. Paul's aunt, Mrs Chick, and her friend, Miss Tox, look on.

COMMENTARY: The reader catches something of the mood of fantasy of *Dombey and Son* from the novel's opening pages. Instead of being a realistic, complex character, Paul's father is a merchant totally absorbed in doing what merchants do, a man to whom the arrival of a son is the ful-filment of the prophecy contained in the name of his business: Dombey and Son. He has no time for his wife, or for his older child, a daughter now six years old. Dreams do fill his mind, but they are dreams of the glorious destiny of his house of trade. In his mind, servants and female relations move like shadows on a busy street. They are of no earthly significance.

Dombey's wife is dying, and his sister seems set fair to make herself the real mistress of the house, with the servile aid of her friend Miss Tox. Poor Miss Tox shows the first signs of infatuation with the august Mr Dombey. As the busy emotions of hope and planning occupy the people downstairs, a sad letting-go takes place upstairs. Mrs Dombey slowly drifts towards death, her frightened daughter embracing her to the last.

NOTES AND GLOSSARY:

sonorous:	resonant
aquiline:	prominent, like the beak of an eagle; often used to describe a nose

---

Chapter 2: In Which Timely Provision is Made for an Emergency That Will Sometimes Arise in the Best-Regulated Families

---

Mrs Polly Toodle is hired by the Dombeys to nurse young Paul on con-dition that she allows herself to be called Richards. Dombey insists with characteristic coldness, that she must not visit Paul once her period of employment is over.

COMMENTARY: This almost comical scene between Mrs Chick, Mr Dombey's sister, and her irrepressibly cheerful husband, follows on the dark comedy of death. The child needs a wet-nurse to replace his dead mother and Mr Chick's bright suggestion of doing 'something temporary... with a teapot' is greeted with haughty disdain. Dickens takes time to assure the reader that the husband is 'often in the ascend-ant himself' and 'In their matrimonial bickerings they were, upon the whole, a well-matched, fairly-balanced, give-and-take couple.' How busy and colourful life seems against the bleak backdrop of death as Miss Tox arrives with not just a potential nurse, but the good woman's entire family, ready for Dombey's inspection. They parade willingly and with good humour.

Mr Dombey's pride in young Paul has been daunted by his wife's death. He finds the selection of a nurse gives him at least the cold plea-sure of rejecting the unsuitable. Although he eventually accepts Mrs Toodle, he insists, curiously, that she calls herself Richards while she is in the house, and that she see her own family as little as possible, and finally that she accept that when Paul ceases to need her she will end all relations with the Dombeys.

When she accepts the post, with a little extra in wages to recompense her loss of her own name, she also has new clothes foisted upon her, mourning for a woman she has never met. Dombey reconciles himself to her presence as well as he can. Mrs Chick and Miss Tox profess themselves well satisfied. The rest of the Toodles seem downcast over the bargain as they depart tearfully.

NOTES AND GLOSSARY:

Mantua-makers:	makers of ladies' loose-bodied overdresses; dress-makers
indecorum:	impropriety

Chapter 3: In Which Mr Dombey, As a Man and a Father, Is Seen at the Head of the Home-Department

---

Florence finds a friend in Polly Toodle, who persuades Mr Dombey to allow Florence to play with her baby brother.

COMMENTARY: The house, in a metaphor of Dombey's preoccupations elsewhere, is now nearly empty. Whole rooms are sealed up, their furniture covered with white 'winding-sheets'. The house gives little invitation to any heart to relax and open to affection. Yet people live there. In its bleak shadows a little girl tries to play and to help to care for her younger brother. The street she sees from her nursery window is respectably quiet, almost deathly quiet. Mr Dombey's own quarters enclose an even more secluded privacy. He keeps three rooms for himself. They face the garden, which he does not enter. From the glass cocoon of a conservatory he looks out on Richards wheeling Paul about, without touching his child or speaking to him.

Richards has had the sad duty of explaining the meaning of death to Florence. She does her best to instil in Florence confidence in her mother's continued love, and a hope that they may be re-united in after-life. Susan Nipper, Florence's pert little maid, really loves Florence, and although she is more a big sister than a mother, she is someone from whom Florence can learn the loyalty, courage, and good sense which daily life requires. This theme, that women interpret and experience life more deeply than men, runs through *Dombey and Son*. All of the women in *Dombey and Son* are cleverer than the men with whom they are involved, despite the fact that men dominate their world. They lead more complex lives than the men of the novel because they have a wider range of social relations. The wise characters of the book are all women, although there are good characters among the men as well. Male goodness for Dickens seems to be linked with a natural simplicity of heart; female goodness seems to be kindness learned through practical experience, a nurturing tenderness toward life that awakens great respect in the reader.

This is not the usual view Dickens takes of women. Although later novels do contain characters such as Agnes Wickfield of *David Copperfield* or Lucie Manette of *A Tale of Two Cities*, or Esther Summerson of *Bleak House*, all of whom the reader is meant to admire, he can seldom feel the depth of genuine admiration he will come to feel for Florence. She is not only good, she is extremely resilient. She is not only innocent, but penetratingly thoughtful. She is not the angel who comforts a male hero, but a young girl whose energy is at the centre of the action.

NOTES AND GLOSSARY:
captious: fault-finding
propitiation: expiation

Chapter 4: In Which Some More First Appearances Are Made on the Stage of These Adventures

---

Walter's first day at work is celebrated with his uncle and Captain Cuttle in a little party.

COMMENTARY: In this chapter the reader is introduced to a snug little household, where the cheery atmosphere of affectionate camaraderie is the very opposite of the gloomy pomp in Dombey's dwelling. Here three friends are meeting, a ship's instrument maker, his young nephew, and an old sea-captain. Uncle and nephew live together. Each feels a great responsibility toward the other; each likes the other with an uncomplicated mutual respect that allows them to share interests in a natural and convincing way. They do indeed rejoice in a common romance, love for the sea, although neither works on a boat. Tall tales make the back parlour a place of wonder and almost by magic the shop itself seems to have taken on a ship's character over the years. Dickens describes Sol Gills, the instrument maker, as going regularly aloft to bed every night in a howling garret remote from the lodgers, where, when gentlemen of England who lived below at ease had little or no idea of the state of the weather, it often blew great guns, with violent force.

Their friend is a true old salt, with a hook for a right hand, and a great many adventures behind him that can only be imagined, as he is normally quite silent. Just occasionally, however, he bursts into speech:

'Wal'r!' he said, arranging his hair (which was thin), with his hook, and then pointing it at the Instrument-maker, 'Look at him!

Love! Honour! And Obey! Overhaul your catechism till you find that passage, and when found turn the leaf down. Success, my boy!'

It is Walter's first day working for Dombey and Son, and his Uncle Sol toasts his success, even hopefully invoking Dick Whittington's success as a happy omen. So the three remember Whittington marrying his master's daughter, and laughingly toast Dombey and Son–and daughter. Walter, however, is able to tell them wistfully that Mr Dombey's daughter is scorned by her father, and is unlikely to make any man's fortune.

NOTES AND GLOSSARY:

clambering: climbing by catching hold with hands and feet

Chapter 5: Paul's Progress and Christening

Paul is christened and the Dombey household celebrates.

COMMENTARY: In this chapter the wars within the Dombey household become more apparent. Florence has her defenders in Richards and the redoubtable Miss Nipper, but she also has detractors, who almost delight in sighing over her misfortunes. Miss Tox and Mrs Chick agree that she has 'poor Fanny's nature' and that she will never win her father's love.

Paul's christening becomes an iron exercise of Dombey's bleak pride. Miss Tox is chosen as godmother because her low station will ensure that young Paul will not turn to a godmother for worldly help. Mr Chick is godfather, as he is by marriage a member of the Dombey family. The gloomy service is almost comic, its macabre touches are so ludicrous. Mr Chick cheers the waiting company by reading aloud the plan of the burial vaults, including the mention of Mrs Dombey's tomb; Miss Tox is unable to concentrate and reads only bits of the service about the Gunpowder Plot. The curate is a ghostly figure in white. Dickens piles up the tiny effects to create a room cluttered up with images of death.

The dreadful party afterwards is only relieved by Dombey's stiff effort to convey gratitude to Richards. He promises her eldest son a place in the Charitable Grinders' School. The image of her little boy in uniform so distresses Polly's mind that she allows Susan Nipper to persuade her to go on a forbidden visit to her own children.

NOTES AND GLOSSARY:

collation: light meal

Chapter 6: Paul's Second Deprivation

Polly visits her family. Florence is lost, and is rescued by Walter Gay.

COMMENTARY: As Polly goes home, she takes the reader into a devastated part of the changing city. A railway line is cutting into Stagg's Gardens, throwing up mud and temporary buildings, like some monster spitting out rubble. Stagg's Gardens itself is a busy neighbourhood buzzing with humble activities, quite incredulous that the monster should care to pass its way.

Polly's family are overjoyed to see her. They soon make Florence, Susan and young Paul quite at home, and the hours pass quickly. A particular route home is chosen so that they can encounter the about-to-be-educated child making his sorry way home from school. Ill luck causes Polly to see her son in a fight. She rushes to the rescue, at the same moment as a carriage careers along the road nearly hitting Susan, Florence and Paul. Startled, Florence runs off, and gets lost in the strange streets. An evil-looking old woman brings her to a hovel, takes off all her pretty clothes and gives her rags. She nearly cuts off her curls as well, but spares them in a mad grief over her own daughter, gone 'beyond seas'. She then releases the child near Dombey's offices, where Florence chances to ask her way from a man who deals with the firm. He sends for Walter Gay, the instrument-maker's nephew, and tells Walter to escort Florence back to her father. By now the offices are closed, but they chance to meet Mr Carker the Junior, a frightened gentleman who also works for Dombey. They consult, and decide that Florence and Walter should go to Walter's uncle's, and Walter should then proceed to Dombey's house, to tell the household Florence is safe, but needs fresh clothing. This plan is effected, as Carker trails them quietly through the shadows. Florence falls peacefully asleep in the instrument-maker's shop, even before Walter can set off for Dombey's.

When he bursts into Dombey's home, a chilly scene greets him; Dombey is angry with Polly and Susan, and almost angry with Walter, for they have all disturbed his majestic solitude. When Walter gets home, he finds quite a different scene. Florence is awake and refreshed, full of lively affection and gratitude. Florence innocently kisses Walter good-bye, and he looks after her carriage with great tenderness. Florence gets home in time to witness Polly's dismissal. She and baby Paul cry long into the night.

Dickens suggests brilliantly how full of people a child's world is; anyone with any right to a child's attention is sure to have it. Adults give very little notice to many people they meet, and some, like Dombey, inhabit a lonely social pinnacle.

Chapter 7: A Bird's-eye Glimpse of Miss Tox's Dwelling-place; Also of the State of Miss Tox's Affections

This chapter describes two of the minor characters, Major Bagstock and Lucretia Tox. They live in the same modest little back street called Princess Place. The descriptions in this chapter are leisurely, but they deepen the novel's seriousness; its minor characters are not just cartoons.

COMMENTARY: One of the people of whom Dombey takes little notice now receives the author's full attention. Miss Tox lives in a house that is the very image of her state in life.

She inhabits a dark little house that had been squeezed, at some remote period of English history, into a fashionable neighbourhood at the west end of the town, where it stands in the shade like a poor relation of the great street round the corner, coldly looked down upon by mighty mansions.

Although really having the status of a servant, Miss Tox flatters herself that she is a friend to the Dombeys, and maybe someday will be something more . . . Yet Dickens shows her guilty only of the innocent old-maid's vanity, in which relationships are magnified because so few are possible.

There is a far more serious flaw in the character of her military neighbour, Major Joseph Bagstock. He huffs and puffs with a wheezing self-regard that is almost brutal in its force. Major Bagstock pursues Miss Tox with an aimless gallantry which is meant to arouse her ardour and gratify his vanity. Her interest is now taken up by the Dombeys, and the Major is much offended. He is more astounded when he sees a baby arriving regularly at her house, accompanied by one or more other ladies. Mid-nineteenth century social uncertainties about class and the limited fluidity of movement from one class to another are captured in this chapter, and are linked to one of the book's themes: old order decaying in a period of brutal economic upheavals.

NOTES AND GLOSSARY:

Mews: a range of stables and coach-houses built around an open space

hostlers: ostlers; men who look after horses at a stable

Chapter 8: Paul's Further Progress, Growth and Character

Paul grows to school age and goes to board at Mrs Pipchin's in Brighton. Florence accompanies him.

COMMENTARY: Paul begins to grow up in the shadows of loneliness. Like a young plant which cannot thrive without sunlight, Paul grows slowly and without strength. His new nurse does not replace Polly in his affections, and he seems to drift away from life despite his father's proud hope that he will occupy a great position when he becomes a man. His father wants him to be a centre of action and energy, but does not give him the emotional energy that would warm his heart and stir him to his best efforts. Dickens describes Paul as having 'an old face' and being like 'one of those terrible little Beings in the Fairy tales, who, at a hundred and fifty or two hundred years of age, fantastically represent the children for whom they have been substituted'. Paul is allowed to sit by the fire with his Papa, a privilege never given to Florence. Their conversations are stiff and odd, but often deep. On one sad evening Paul asks his father what money can do and why it didn't save his Mama. He adds then that it cannot make him well and strong. Dombey is alarmed. He checks Paul's health the next day and finds that the doctor has recommended sea-air. Miss Tox and Mrs Chick come forward with the suggestion of a Mrs Pipchin's boarding-school at Brighton. They recommend that he should go there with Florence and his new nurse.

Mrs Pipchin is a firm-minded widow whose views on children are to 'give them everything that they didn't like, and nothing that they did'. She and Paul strike up a frank relationship from the start when he tells her the house is nasty and he will not like it at all. They attract each other; Dickens says Mrs Pipchin is witch-like, and Paul seems like a witch's cat.

Paul's oddity, however, takes another more alarming form as time goes on. He needs to be wheeled in a small carriage on his outings; he best likes sitting by the rolling sea, with only his sister's company. 'The sea . . . what is it that it keeps on saying,' he asks her; 'What place is over there?' The far place beyond life is calling Paul home.

NOTES AND GLOSSARY:
reverberation: echo
multifarious: many and various

Chapter 9: In Which the Wooden Midshipman Gets Into Trouble

The folk at The Wooden Midshipman face an alarming financial crisis, and appeal to Mr Dombey for help.

COMMENTARY: Dickens changes the atmosphere completely here, giving the reader a break from the strange melancholy that would otherwise become monotonous. The chapter takes up the life of Walter Gay; the eccentricity of Walter's uncle has nearly brought the little shop to ruin. The truth can no longer be concealed from young Walter, who, as soon as he learns it, turns to Captain Cuttle for advice. That kind-spirited man puts forward his own 'property' as part-payment, but the creditor is mightily unimpressed. Gills has some money invested, but he cannot get it readily. His only practical plan is to close his shop and sell all his stock. This terrible defeat is only warded off by the Captain's suggestion that he and Walter should appeal to Mr Dombey to advance the money, as a loan. Dombey is in Brighton, so they set off for Brighton together.

NOTES AND GLOSSARY:
non-Dominical: not falling on a Sunday

Chapter 10: Containing the Sequel of the Midshipman's Disaster

Mr Dombey and Major Bagstock become friendly.

COMMENTARY: Major Bagstock is also under way, steering in the direction of Brighton. He wishes to meet his great rival for Miss Tox's approving gaze, the imperious Mr Dombey. Bagstock has a strategy; he will visit the son of an old comrade, a young Master Bitherstone, who is a schoolfellow of Paul Dombey. While he is in possession of this youngster, Bagstock manages to encounter Mr Dombey and Paul. A big dose of flattery does the rest; he and Dombey part on excellent terms, having agreed to meet again.

After describing this blossoming false friendship, Dickens returns to the steadfast young Walter Gay. Walter and Captain Cuttle arrive at the Dombey house, and are welcomed by Florence. They are ushered into Mr Dombey's presence, where Walter pleads for help for his uncle. Mr Dombey turns to Paul to ask if he wishes the money to be lent. Paul says he does, with a heartfelt sympathy for Walter and for Florence, who regards Walter fondly.

Walter feels that this debt must create a gulf between himself and Florence. Captain Cuttle and Florence take a different view; they feel it brings the pair closer together.

A child without a future, who lives in a solitary world with only a few close friendships, can never bring any substantial hope to Mr Dombey's ambitions. In this chapter, however, Paul comes as close to being Mr Dombey's child as he ever will. He enjoys what money can do; the touch of power enlivens him for a moment, and he and his father share that, even though they would disagree about the proper use of money.

NOTES AND GLOSSARY:
inflammatory: quick to flare up
eulogising: praising to excess

Chapter 11: Paul's Introduction to a New Scene

This chapter describes Paul's life at Mrs Pipchin's. A year later, Paul is enrolled in Dr Blimber's academy.

COMMENTARY: Mrs Pipchin is shown as the grotesque character she is, both in her petty cruelties to her niece and in her strange relationship with Paul. Paul and she share a devastating mutual honesty; a truce exists between them. Paul is free of her tyranny because she cannot frighten him. She only interests him. He views her as a departing guest can view a landlord, with a disinterested, somewhat pleasurable curiosity.

Paul is to leave Mrs Pipchin's care and begin serious studies at Dr Blimber's school nearby. He will be a weekly boarder there, and so will be able to visit Florence on Saturdays. Dr Blimber, Dickens tells the reader, gave ten scholars enough knowledge for one hundred till their poor heads could hold no more. His eldest student is Toots, a genial boy approaching manhood, with the bright hope of forgetting most of what he has learned.

Paul is plunged into sorrow and loneliness at this separation from Florence. He feels too weary to begin study and too small to tackle life alone. Although his captors are not very harsh people, he feels a prisoner whose only parole is his weekend visits to Florence.

NOTES AND GLOSSARY:
soporific:	sleep-inducing
bombazeen:	a twilled dress fabric, made of silk or cotton, and worsted

Chapter 12: Paul's Education

Paul is introduced to his fellow pupils and is given a great many books to read.

COMMENTARY: Paul's first examination goes badly. He only wants to see old Glubb, a man who used to take him down to the sea. He has no desire to learn anything except why the sea always makes him think of his dead mama and what it is always saying. He meets the other boys, who, Dickens says, are in various degrees of mental prostration; they are abjectly dull, but not unfriendly. The studies Paul undertakes come at him like a hailstorm of facts, quite beating him down.

Florence, now established with Susan Nipper at Mrs Pipchin's, is faring better. Her studies are not such a burden, and she undertakes Paul's as well, to be of help to him. With her assistance, Paul can make respectable progress.

But he daydreams his young life away in his free time and seems more and more solitary. His hold on life weakens, except for his love of Florence. Florence cares for Paul intensely. She passes under his window at a certain time each evening, to wave to him. On Saturdays their father watches, hidden; he no longer tries to share their world.

NOTES AND GLOSSARY:

orthography: spelling

Chapter 13: Shipping Intelligence and Office Business

This chapter deepens the reader's awareness of Dombey's character by showing his only creation, the firm of Dombey and Son. The reader also meets Mr Carker, another main character.

COMMENTARY: The reader follows Mr Dombey's stately progress to his office. Having seen the children's school world, and the cold world of the Dombey household, the reader is offered a look at Dombey's place of business, sharing Dickens's sense of oppression and incomprehension. Dickens always keeps this childlike view of the office alive in his reader's imagination by having young Walter Gay work there.

Mr Dombey is the gloomy mainspring of this clockwork world, where people always minutely follow a routine dictated by his mere presence. No spontaneity enlivens or alters this routine. A reader will sense that the all-too-willing, all-too-helpful Mr Carker the manager is tinkering with this clock. Yet flattery conceals his scheming from Mr Dombey. He seems eager to oblige. Mr Dombey, on a whim of annoyance, appoints Walter Gay to a post in the West Indies. Carker ushers Walter in and out of Dombey's presence, as if only Mr Dombey's pleasure were at stake in this decision.

John Carker, the manager's brother, has a private interview in which Carker-the-successful berates Carker-the-downtrodden, for bringing disgrace to the family, and suggests that his friendship with Walter will do the boy nothing but harm. Walter overhears this, with amazement, and defends John Carker spiritedly, but is scorned by Carker's brother, and sees only sorrow in the other man's face. A tale of some past disgrace seems to hover in the air. Later Mr John Carker privately tells Walter that he once robbed the firm, and now must serve, year in and year out, a penance of servitude and humiliation. Walter's own sorrows also crowd in upon the young boy's imagination: he must leave home, and leave behind all hopes of a closer link with Florence.

NOTES AND GLOSSARY:

officiously: in a manner that offers services that are neither requested nor needed

Chapter 14: Paul Grows More and More Old-fashioned and Goes Home for the Holidays

The reader now begins to take leave of Paul in the sorrowful aura of the death of an innocent.

COMMENTARY: In this chapter Dickens centres the reader's feelings on young Paul as he slips away from life toward death. Even the school reports that worry the other boys so much do not upset Paul. The only phrase in his report which puzzles him is that he is 'old-fashioned', a term which keeps recurring in different people's description of him. A serious directness, a profound and unshakeable innocence, and a deep sense of the unimportance, for him, of advancing upon adult life with the means of succeeding in it, seem to compound the quality which other people find so striking in him. Paul simply involves himself more and more in emotional life: his human relationships are all carefully put in good order, as he prepares to take his leave of Dr Blimber's school. Most of the boys become quite fond of him, and even the Doctor and Cornelia show signs of weakening. His special friend is the amiable Mr Toots, who will soon come into his property and end his education. There is between them a special bond of innocence; the strains of school life have hurt them, but have not at all impaired their characters.

Blimber's establishment closes formally with an end-of-term evening party, to which special visitors are invited. Florence creates a gentle sensation by her beauty and her winning good nature. She is much more sophisticated than Paul; she sings for the company although her heart is breaking to see her little brother so ill. In every way she demonstrates intelligence and energy of character, although Dickens allows her no central role except that which she has in Paul's heart.

At the chapter's close, Paul is back home lying in bed and wondering if he has heard his father weeping. Dickens will now change the subject, leaving the reader to feel a tender concern for the dying child, while he portrays the hustle and bustle of life elsewhere.

NOTES AND GLOSSARY:

Quadrille: a quadrille is a square dance for four couples, or the music for it (the word can also mean a four-handed card game)

Chapter 15: Amazing Artfulness of Captain Cuttle, and a New Pursuit for Walter Gay

This chapter belongs to the good characters. Walter and Captain Cuttle decide to break the news of Walter's new post to Sol Gills;

Walter thinks about leaving Florence and is suddenly caught up in her life again, as Susan Nipper asks him to help her find Polly Toodle.

COMMENTARY: The novel now turns to another circle of whom the reader is perhaps fond—the folk who foregather at The Wooden Midshipman. Walter is puzzling over how to tell his Uncle Sol that he must leave him for Barbados. He seeks out Captain Cuttle, to ask for advice. To him he frankly confesses that Mr Dombey may be sending him away to get rid of him. The Captain sadly agrees to break the news to Walter's uncle, and they decide to put it in as favourable a light as possible. To this, Captain Cuttle adds, with the best intentions, a secret scheme to have a word with Mr Dombey about the real merits of Walter.

As he walks about waiting for Cuttle to conclude the business with Sol, Walter finds he is a little in love with Florence. It is a youthful, idealised love:

> In a word, Walter found out that to reason with himself about Florence at all was to become very unreasonable indeed, and that he could do no better than preserve her image in his mind as something precious, unattainable, unchangeable, and indefinite—indefinite in all but its power of giving him pleasure, and restraining him like an angel's hand from anything unworthy.

This reverie is interrupted comically and yet sadly by Susan Nipper. She arrives in a coach; she is wildly upset and asks Walter to help her to find Stagg's Gardens. She explains that poor Paul wants to see his old nurse Polly once more, but that she cannot find her house.

The arrival of the railway has totally altered Polly's neighbourhood. It is now busy and prosperous, bristling with dozens of new chimneys along its skyline. The Toodles are enjoying occupancy of a new home owned by the railway company, as Mr Toodles now works as an engine fireman.

Walter and Susan bring Polly to Paul, so it is not Captain Cuttle alone who pays a call on the Dombeys that sad day.

NOTES AND GLOSSARY:

gimlet: a small tool with a sharp point for boring holes
puncheons: wine casks

Chapter 16: What the Waves Were Always Saying

This chapter tells the reader about Paul's death.

COMMENTARY: Paul's mind constantly turns to the image of the dark river, rushing on toward the sea. He lies quietly in bed, but sometimes in his fancy he is trying to stop the river, alone. Then he calls for Florence, who always comes to him.

Paul's father visits his room often, and watches sadly. Paul tries to comfort him. Paul calls for his old nurse, and is delighted to see her; he begs her to stay with him. Then he calls for Walter, to whom he says simply, 'Good-bye'. Then he says to his father, 'Remember Walter, dear Papa . . . Remember Walter. I was fond of Walter!'

Lastly he asks Florence to hold him. As she does he tells her the river is reaching the sea. But once at sea, he tells her, he sees another green shore, and someone on the bank.

> 'Mama is like you, Floy. I know her by the face! But tell them that the print upon the stairs at the school is not divine enough. The light about the head is shining on me as I go!'

Dickens ends the chapter in a declaration of faith:

> The golden ripple on the wall came back again, and nothing else stirred in the room. The old, old fashion! The fashion that came in with our first garments, and will last unchanged until our race has run its course, and the wide firmament is rolled up like a scroll. The old, old fashion—Death!
>
> Oh, thank GOD, all who see it, for that older fashion yet, of Immortality! And look upon us, angels of young children, with regards not quite estranged, when the swift river bears us to the ocean!

NOTES AND GLOSSARY:
estranged: alienated

Chapter 17: Captain Cuttle Does a Little Business for the Young People

---

Captain Cuttle calls on Mr Carker, and is duped by him.

COMMENTARY: In the previous chapter Dickens has been showing the natural, seemingly inevitable, link between the Dombeys and Walter which all the good characters seem instinctively to sense.

Now, in an almost comic chapter, Dickens demonstrates the obstacles to Walter's progress, both the simplicity of his friends and the casual malice of his enemies. Both Captain Cuttle and Sol Gills become reconciled to Walter's imminent departure under the delusion that he will prosper in Barbados. Walter has little time for grief. He has only two weeks before the ship sets sail. This knowledge spurs the Captain to renewed efforts on Walter's behalf. He calls on Mr Dombey's manager, Mr Carker. Mr Carker easily deceives the Captain as to Gay's 'brilliant prospects'. Why he bothers to do so remains something of a mystery.

NOTES AND GLOSSARY:
sagacity: wisdom

Chapter 18: Father and Daughter

Paul is buried and Florence is spurned by her father. Mr Toots calls and gives Florence the dog Diogenes, Paul's friend at Brighton.

COMMENTARY: In contrast to all the bustle surrounding Walter, a deathly hush pervades Mr Dombey's residence. The sad panoply of a child's funeral disturbs the terrible emptiness of that house only a little; then the church receives young Paul, and gives him over to God. Florence grieves alone; her father scarcely remembers her existence. He even requests a memorial tablet for Paul to be inscribed 'beloved and only child'. Florence grieves for her one friend and companion with a devastating sense of loss, but Dickens shows she has the strength to bear her grief with dignity. He gives her a strength Paul never had.

In her sorrow she reaches out again to her father, but Mrs Chick, her aunt, warns her against disturbing him. Miss Tox is genuinely moved by Florence's bravery and suffering. She begins to emerge from the shadow of her friend Mrs Chick, to experience and demonstrate emotional attitudes of her own. The loyal Susan Nipper is Florence's best comforter, and the gentle ghost of Paul seems to convince her that he is alive in some new and joyous world.

Mr Toots arrives to comfort her, bringing with him the clumsy old dog from Blimper's as a present for her. Mr Dombey, on the other hand, prepares to depart on holiday without a word to her. Florence seeks him out, but is rebuffed, as if she had been Paul's rival, and not his nurturing and affectionate friend. As the chapter closes Florence, not yet fourteen, is a young woman in her solitude and self-reliance.

NOTES AND GLOSSARY:
disparaged: spoke slightingly of

Chapter 19: Walter Goes Away

Walter leaves for Barbados, after saying a warm good-bye to his friends, and pledging a brother's love to Florence.

COMMENTARY: Walter is leaving The Wooden Midshipman, but the affections of that little company are never livelier than in the saddening last days together. Florence is not forgotten, either. Walter leaves a request with Susan, that news of Florence be sent to his uncle from time to time. It is one of Dickens's happiest thoughts that good people attract each other and are seldom alone for long. With this he contrasts the terrible isolation of hidden wrong-doing, which by its very nature isolates the culprit from his fellows.

Just as Walter is speaking of Florence to his uncle, she and Susan Nipper arrive. They pass a tender hour together. Florence asks Walter to be her adopted brother. For Walter, who is older, it is a sacrifice as well as a delight to be in the position of her brother only, but he agrees nonetheless. Florence promises to visit Walter's uncle regularly, and she and Susan settle comfortable and naturally into the circle of friends at The Wooden Midshipman. As Walter escorts her to her coach, they speak of his new appointment to Barbados, and quickly come to understand that both are banished from the powerful Mr Dombey's regard. She gives him a parting gift of a hand-made purse with a bit of money in it.

The next day, Captain Cuttle arrives to say his farewell. It is decided by the company that the last special bottle of Madeira will be kept against the day of Walter's return.

Mr Carker Junior also arrives to wish Walter well. Time passes relentlessly and at last young Walter Gay must go to the docks, board the *Son and Heir* and sail away.

NOTES AND GLOSSARY:
unimpeachable: blameless, irreproachable
modulation: change of tone

Chapter 20: Mr Dombey Goes upon a Journey

Dombey takes a holiday with Major Bagstock.

COMMENTARY: In one of the many breaks in the narrative, by which Dickens hopes to sustain his readers' curiosity, this chapter takes the reader away from Walter's circle, to Mr Dombey and his false friend, his friend of convenience, Major Joseph Bagstock. The reader can never forget that the Major first sought out Dombey from idle pique and vanity. He wanted to meet his rival for Miss Tox's affectionate esteem and to eclipse him. Bagstock, however, cares little for Miss Tox, and that first motive is almost forgotten by him now. He now pursues Dombey for the gratification of being Dombey's friend and sharing in the aura of riches and power that Dombey generates. However, as the occasion arises, Bagstock belittles Miss Tox to Dombey and paints her as an ambitious and artful jade, aiming at marriage to Mr Dombey. Dombey is disgusted.

At the railway station Bagstock and Dombey are approached by Mr Toodle, husband to Paul's first nurse, whom Dombey had rechristened Richards. Toodle offers his condolences to Dombey who, however, resents this. Dombey is in a strange state of mind in which all those who shared Paul's brief life arouse his envy. His loss has angered him, and the envy he feels is poisoned by contempt for others, and a deep desire to rid himself of all reminders that Paul was not solely his. Most tormenting of all is his memory of Florence, whose appeal for his love offends him deeply, almost physically.

NOTES AND GLOSSARY:

levee: a morning reception held by a person of great distinction

Chapter 21: New Faces

Dombey meets Edith Granger, and finds her attractive.

COMMENTARY: This chapter marks the entrance of a new group of acquaintances, ushered in by an introduction from Major Bagstock. An elderly flirt named Mrs Skewton and her widowed daughter, Mrs Granger, who live mainly 'upon the reputation of some diamonds and ... family connexions'. A frail and ghastly show of worldly panoply almost frightens the reader, but seems to attract Dombey, and Bagstock. A vestige of eighteenth-century wealthy artificiality, making a flourish toward early nineteenth-century Romanticism, is Mrs Skewton's cardboard-character gesture toward the business of living. Her daughter's attitude is one of perpetual universal contempt which Mr Dombey finds very congenial, and almost challenging. He and Major Bagstock spend pleasant hours in the ladies' company. Though he cannot soften Edith Granger's attitude Mr Dombey continues to find her appealing.

NOTES AND GLOSSARY:

insensibility: lack of feeling

Chapter 22: A Trifle of Management by Mr Carker the Manager

Mr Carker employs Rob Toodle. Mr Toots calls on Florence.

COMMENTARY: The crafty Carker is at work while Dombey is on holiday. In him Dickens again portrays the solitude of selfishness, which is one of the book's principal themes. Although Dickens is not normally thought of as a particularly Christian writer, this book is full of Christian paradoxes; the seemingly weak are strong, the pure of heart are ultimately defended from evil by what they are, by their inner strength and the love they inspire in others. The proud are sent away empty. Sin is a lonely and terrible business in Dickens's view. Even as Mr Carker enjoys his machinations, the very isolation that will ultimately destroy him envelops him completely.

Carker takes an interest in Biler Toodle and decides that he would be a good lackey. He has a naturally idle, cowardly nature; he is willing to spy on people but easy to manage, as he has no personal initiative. In his turn, Biler admires Carker's ruthlessness. Carker gives Biler over to Sol Gills, in nearly the same breath as he accepts Sol's loan repayment and informs him there is no news of the *Son and Heir*.

Meanwhile in a comic scene, Dickens shows the reader the faithful Mr Toots calling on Florence Dombey, though too shy to do more than present a visiting card, almost daily, with his compliments. Seized by a sudden inspiration, Toots kisses Susan Nipper but is attacked by the ever-faithful Diogenes.

NOTES AND GLOSSARY:

purport:	meaning
chivied:	chased
emulation:	ambition to rival or surpass another

Chapter 23: Florence Solitary, and the Midshipman Mysterious

Florence realises Walter may be lost at sea and calls on Walter's friends.

COMMENTARY: Florence has been left for some months to live quietly on her own in the big house. She studies, chats with Susan, plays with Diogenes, and dreams of her father opening his heart to her. A shadow of anxiety about Walter's ship increasingly darkens her life. One day she seeks out Sol Gills, and not finding him at home, ventures to call upon Captain Cuttle. Cuttle determines to bring his friend Bunsby to comfort Sol Gills, so they collect him and go back to the instrument-maker's shop. Sol Gills seems a little wild in his speech, as if he is making a desperate decision.

NOTES AND GLOSSARY:

succedaneum:	substitute
oracular:	resembling an oracle, as in solemnity, wisdom, obscurity, dogmatism

Chapter 24: The Study of a Loving Heart

Florence and Susan visit the Skettles. Florence begins to grow up.

COMMENTARY: Florence and Susan take a summer holiday at the residence of Sir Barnet Skettles. There Florence studies the young children, who talk so happily and easily to their parents, as if to learn from them how to win over her father.

She overhears a friendly voice speaking of her, saying that her father does not love her, but that she is not to blame for his coldness. Her courage deserts her for a moment as she hears the speaker say 'not an orphan in the wide world can be so deserted as the child who is an outcast from a living parent's love'. However, her courage and resolution return. She is becoming a remarkable woman, generous and thoughtful, resolute and methodical. Her goodness will become a force to be reckoned with; it is not the delicate flower of Dickens's usual girl characters, but a strong force of kindliness which brings a nurturing warmth and a fresh vitality to all it touches.

One sad day Carker calls, to say he is going down to Leamington to see Dombey, and to ask if Florence has any message for him. Only her love—and that unwanted.

NOTES AND GLOSSARY:
sensible: aware
divining: guessing, understanding

Chapter 25: Strange News of Uncle Sol

Sol Gills disappears, leaving a letter for Captain Cuttle, along with his will.

COMMENTARY: The faintly comic portrayal of Captain Cuttle's real sorrows in this chapter makes what could be disturbing and yet mawkish into a convincing picture of the nature of life: irrepressibly itself even as it goes down. The Captain's friend Sol Gills disappears, leaving a letter and a will. Cuttle fears his friend has killed himself and for a week checks all the local victims of sudden death but cannot find Sol Gill's remains. Then he decides to leave Mrs MacStinger's to take up residence in the old shop as the best way of keeping Walter's home ready for him. But he lives in such fear of discovery by his ex-landlady that he leaves his belongings in a locked chest in her house, and creeps away with a small bundle in the dead of night. Once stowed away in Sol's shop, he hides for most of the daylight hours in a back room, until the weeks lengthen and he feels safe.

NOTES AND GLOSSARY:
tackle: equipment

Chapter 26: Shadows of the Past and Future

Bagstock schemes with Mrs Skewton to marry Edith Granger to Dombey, and reveals his plan to Carker.

COMMENTARY: Dombey has a visit from Carker, who insinuates into their business conversation an ill word about Florence, and extracts the unwelcome information that Dombey is wooing Mrs Granger. While Carker and Dombey consult, the Major bounds off to see Mrs Skewton, and they have a ridiculous conversation about Edith's love for Dombey. It is arranged that all will meet the next day. The three men pass the evening together. Major Bagstock and Carker talk to each other, each feeling sly and capable. Dombey remains proud and aloof, although the willing subject of their conversations. Carker's evil heart is shown clearly to the reader as the chapter ends, with his private fantasy of power.

NOTES AND GLOSSARY:

tropical:	hot-blooded and full of passion
rallying:	teasing
cravat:	a neckcloth

Chapter 27: Deeper Shadows

Edith frets about her forthcoming marriage. She confronts her mother. Her bondage to Carker begins.

COMMENTARY: Edith Granger's sorrow over her forthcoming marriage is vivid in her own mind, but seemingly invisible to Bagstock or Dombey. Carker, the evil Manager, catches her weeping, and from then on knows she is betraying herself into this unholy wedlock. Edith fights with her mother over the deed they have done together, the luring of a rich lover into the bondage of marriage. In the rest of the novel Dickens will (perhaps partly from his own unhappy experience) re-create the intense misery of an unhappy marriage. Neither Edith nor Dombey have any intention of yielding anything to the other. Worse still they are witnessed in their pride by an enemy whose deepest desire is that they should destroy each other.

NOTES AND GLOSSARY:

propensity:	inclination, tendency
cumbrous:	unwieldy, clumsy

Chapter 28: Alterations

Florence returns home to a house in confusion as preparations are being made for Dombey's marriage. She meets Edith Granger.

COMMENTARY: The other woman closely involved with Dombey is the centre of this chapter. This is Florence, for she seems to be no longer a girl. Like Edith Granger, she senses Carker's evil interest in her affairs, and shivers at it.

She comes home after an extended visit to the Skettleses, and finds the house in great confusion. It is being redecorated for Dombey's new wife. Poor Florence knows nothing of the intended marriage until her father brusquely introduces her to Edith. Florence bursts into tears and Edith embraces her gently. Then she asks her most earnestly to begin their new relationship by trusting her. Florence warmly agrees to do so.

NOTES AND GLOSSARY:

bridled:	held up [her] head as if in pique and pride
hypothetical:	imagined, for the sake of argument

Chapter 29: The Opening of the Eyes of Mrs Chick

Miss Tox is told of Dombey's impending marriage. Her distress offends Mrs Chick, Dombey's sister.

COMMENTARY: Dickens returns to Miss Tox, more sympathetically than in any previous chapter. She is more of a character and less of a caricature than ever before. Her maidenly fondness for caged birds and potted plants, for life well under control, is faintly disturbed by an admiration for Mr Dombey that is a little romantic.

Mrs Chick arrives, interrupting her reverie with a baleful desultory conversation that can only bode ill. Ill news indeed it does bring; when she eventually divulges her brother's intention of marrying, poor Miss Tox faints. Her former friend takes offence. Does she dare to suppose she has something to faint about? Mrs Chick, thus morally outraged, denies that she ever encouraged Miss Tox to hope Mr Dombey could be interested in her, and storms off. The sketch of a woman's friendship blighted by confused match-making is not subtle, but funny and somewhat poignant.

NOTES AND GLOSSARY:

viands:	food
exordium:	introduction to an oration

Chapter 30: The Interval before the Marriage

Edith and Florence become fond of each other.

COMMENTARY: The new triangle of relationships in the Dombey household is shown to the reader. Edith hates Dombey, who has bought her as he would a handsome piece of furniture. She is fiercely protective of Florence, whose innocence rouses her to both shame and anger. Dombey remains cool towards Florence. His admiration of Edith is a chilly one; he cares little whether she loves him or not.

Mrs Skewton is congratulating herself on Edith being well placed, but when she asks for Florence's company, Edith is provoked into forbidding it. She sees herself as almost a prostitute, and will not allow Florence near her corrupter.

In this chapter the book touches, in shadowy darkness, on its central compassionate concern: the ways in which women must achieve their security in the social world of nineteenth-century England. Both happy and unhappy women people the book. Some find the safety and fulfilment they seek, others cannot; but unlike the male characters, the women all seem aware of a need to struggle, and seem touched by a sense of what they have in common with other women.

NOTES AND GLOSSARY:

paroxysm: a fit or emotional convulsion

requisites: that which is required or needful

Chapter 31: The Wedding

Dombey's unhappy marriage begins. Carker watches, menacingly.

COMMENTARY: Edith Granger's marriage to Dombey has all the solemnity of a grave sin unsoftened by the gentle, courteous rites of marriage. Dombey's is a wooden nature compared to Edith's. He acts out the mechanical gestures of habitual pride. She feels consciously trapped by her own past decisions and yet tries to save Florence's innocence in a strange barter that gives the devil her own soul if he will leave Florence untempted. So Florence returns to her solitude, untroubled by anything beyond loneliness.

All the while the menacing figure of Mr Carker is repeatedly pointed out to the reader. Dickens shows us the villain in repose, awaiting his hour for action and enjoying the passive pleasure of power restrained by a gloating patience. Dickens also shows the casual nature of evil revealing how Carker almost collects people he can manipulate, for no obvious reason. He gratifies his secret pride.

NOTES AND GLOSSARY:

portly: dignified and stout

barouche: a four-wheeled carriage with a driver's seat in front, two double seats inside facing each other, and a folding top

hatchments: panels on which the arms of a deceased person are temporarily displayed

Chapter 32: The Wooden Midshipman Goes to Pieces

Mr Toots and Captain Cuttle become acquainted and strike up a friendship, because they both care about Florence. There is no good news of the *Son and Heir*.

COMMENTARY: This sad chapter brings two sympathetic characters together, two faithful souls, Mr Toots and Captain Cuttle. Mr Toots seeks out the Captain, commissioned by Susan Nipper to ask if there is any truth in a newspaper report that the *Son and Heir* went down with all hands. The Captain is eloquent in grief.

'Wal'r, my dear lad,' said the Captain, 'farewell! Wal'r my child, my boy, and man, I loved you! He warn't my flesh and blood,' said the Captain, looking at the fire—'I an't got none—but something of what a father feels when he loses a son, I feel in losing Wal'r. For why?' said the Captain. 'Because it an't one loss, but a round dozen. Where's that there young schoolboy with the rosy face and curly hair, that used to be as merry in this here parlour, come round every week, as a piece of music? Gone down with Wal'r. Where's that there fresh lad that nothing couldn't tire nor put out, and that sparkled up and blushed so when we joked him about Heart's Delight that he was beautiful to look at? Gone down with Wal'r. Where's that there man's spirit, all afire, that wouldn't see the old man hove down for a minute, and cared nothing for itself? Gone down with Wal'r. It an't one Wal'r. There was a dozen Wal'rs that I know'd and loved, all holding round his neck when he went down, and they're a-holding round mine now!'

Mr Toots is inspired to a fever of sympathy, and love of Miss Dombey stirs him to greater fervour in seeking to console the Captain. He begs the Captain to take him for a friend; the Captain, with measured judgment, agrees to consider it.

Captain Cuttle then proceeds to Carker's office for confirmation of the tragic news. Mr Carker's manner is quite a contrast to Toots's, and leads the Captain's slow wits to make another judgment.

'My lad,' returned the Captain, slowly—'you are a'most a lad to me, and so I don't ask your pardon for that slip of a word—if you find any pleasure in this here sport, you an't the gentleman I took you for, and if you an't the gentleman I took you for, may be my mind has call to be uneasy.'

Carker throws the good Captain out, and the reader's sense of the man's innate dignity is strengthened rather than upset. As the chapter closes, the Captain performs his own simple ritual of mourning, an act of love by which any true-hearted reader will be moved.

NOTES AND GLOSSARY:

immured:	imprisoned
suppositious:	hypothetical, imagined
sluicing:	pouring, gushing

Chapter 33: Contrasts

This chapter contrasts the homes of the two Carker brothers. Carker the manager lives in a private world of elegant comfort, whereas John Carker lives humbly with his trusted sister. Carker the manager is usually alone. In this chapter John and Harriet Carker discover a new friend's regard for them.

COMMENTARY: The reader is taken into the private house of Mr Carker, and finds it quite a public place, arranged in a careful display of wealth. It suggests Carker is his own best admirer. Across London is Carker's brother's house, a dull and poor place, patiently kept by his good friend and sister Harriet.

Harriet receives a mysterious caller, who knows her brother's whole history, and yet wishes them both well. The caller wants to stop near their house each week, to see at a distance if all is well. She consents to this strange, yet courteous request. After he has left, she watches the poor folk struggling into London in the cruel winter weather. Outside her cottage Harriet sees a poor woman of her own age overcome by weariness. She brings her in, and helps her to recover. The woman is a reckless beauty, returning to London after years as a convict in Australia. She and the mild Harriet seem attracted to each other and share a simple conversation and a frugal meal, before the woman goes her sorry way.

NOTES AND GLOSSARY:

almanack:	a book or table containing a calendar of days, weeks, and months, to which astronomical data and various statistics are often added
unremitting:	incessant, not stopping

Chapter 34: Another Mother and Daughter

This chapter shows the reader Alice Brown's mother, who urges her daughter to accept ruin and feel hate. Alice, however, shows her more turbulent spirit.

COMMENTARY: The wild woman who stopped at Harriet Carker's now goes home to her mother, 'Good Mrs Brown' (whose real name is Marwood). Their bitter conversation is not very different from Edith's with her mother. But their desperate poverty seems to be relieved by a bond of some kind between them, uniting them despite the daughter's reproaches. The mother has tracked down the man who ruined her daughter: Mr Carker the manager. In seeking him she has learned much of the Dombeys and recounts Edith's sorrow to her daughter

Alice. Dickens pointedly suggests that their sorrows are parallel; they were both groomed by their mothers for sale, and were sold, and will be. The witch – like grotesque women who ruin these younger women seem almost taken from some fairy tale; yet beneath that fantastic picture we feel Dickens's appalled anger, as real as anything expressed by other authors in savage satire.

As Alice listens to her mother she realises Harriet is a sister of the evil Mr Carker. She then insists that they return the small sum of money Harriet had given her, and they walk to the cottage where Alice throws down the money, and curses the family.

NOTES AND GLOSSARY:
mutilated: deformed or scarred by injury

Chapter 35: The Happy Pair

The newly-married Dombeys come home. Edith stiffly rejects Dombey but turns, with respect and even with protective love, toward Florence.

COMMENTARY: The home-coming of Paul and Edith Dombey is a grim one, though Florence and the servants do all they can to make it happy. Edith suffers Dombey's attentions as if she were the unwilling concubine of a conquering potentate. Dombey feels the first chill of failing to own what he thought he was buying.

Florence and Edith are close friends. Florence tells Edith privately that she is carrying two sorrows, her grief for her friend Walter, and her anguish over her father's coldness. Edith comforts her as well as she can, but finally says she cannot help her to a reconciliation with her father. Edith begs Florence, when she comes to her mature years, not to judge her harshly. She promises to cherish Florence as much, if not as well, as any woman could.

While Dombey broods alone downstairs, the two women sit together till Florence falls into a troubled sleep. But in this chapter Dickens gives the first indication that Dombey's finer self can yet be stirred:

But as he looked, he softened to her, more and more. As he looked, she became blended with the child he had loved, and he could hardly separate the two. As he looked, he saw her for an instant by a clearer and brighter light, not bending over that child's pillow as his rival—monstrous thought—but as the spirit of his home, and in the action tending himself no less, as he sat once more with his bowed-down head upon his hand at the foot of the little bed. He felt inclined to speak to her, and call her to him. The words 'Florence, come here!' were rising to his lips—but slowly and with difficulty, they were so very strange—when they were checked and stifled by a footstep on the stair.

NOTES AND GLOSSARY:
saturnine: gloomy
blurred: out of focus

Chapter 36: Housewarming

This chapter describes Dombey's first party, at which he introduces Edith to all his business associates.

COMMENTARY: This chapter describes the dreadful evening of the Dombeys' first dinner party. Old friends of Mrs Skewton share the table with associates of Mr Dombey, and they could not have been more ill-sorted if faded butterflies shared food with keen-eyed hounds. Florence becomes deeply withdrawn. She begins to realise her father's marriage is no blessing.

After the guests have left, but in the presence of Mr Carker, Dombey takes his wife to task. She scorns to reply, and he is silenced. Mrs Skewton and Mr Carker make light of the quarrel, though both fully understand how serious it is. That night Edith visits Florence as usual. That night, as usual, Dombey nurses his wounded pride, alone.

NOTES AND GLOSSARY:
taciturn: habitually silent
ottoman: a flat, overstuffed couch

Chapter 37: More Warnings than One

Edith finds herself deep in trouble. After the quarrel between Dombey and herself in Carker's presence, the latter calls and speaks in a menacing tone of her regard for Florence. That same evening her mother suffers a stroke from which she will only partially recover.

COMMENTARY: Carker calls on Mrs Dombey. Exuding polite menace, he refers to Florence's association with Walter, Captain Cuttle, and Sol Gills as if it were a regrettable indiscretion. He suggests that Dombey should know of it, yet he intimates that such knowledge would, in all probability, lead Dombey to throw Florence out of his house. Perhaps, suggests Carker, it is sufficient to let Mrs Dombey know. Mrs Dombey realises Carker's emotional blackmail will give him great power over her, but for love of Florence, she assumes this heavy burden.

That evening her mother, Mrs Skewton, suffers a stroke. From then on she is a dancing death's head, the very antithesis of life. Mere vanity sustains her, and her soul seems partly to have left her body, leaving it to make its habitual, but now meaningless gestures.

NOTES AND GLOSSARY:

pomatum:	pomade, hair oil
zephyrs:	gentle breezes
apposite:	appropriate

Chapter 38: Miss Tox Improves an Old Acquaintance

Miss Tox returns to social life, and makes real friends of the Toodles. Rob takes a small turn for the worse.

COMMENTARY: Dickens creates a memorable minor character by taking some grotesque impression and elevating it to an eccentric individual trait that defines the way that person sees the world. A man, in Dickens's imaginative writing, might not just have a wooden leg, but a wooden leg on which he etched all his relatives' initials. He might always be on the lookout for new unexpected relations to add to his collection. Yet, just as in real life, other unrelated traits would co-exist in his character, beside this private obsession. He might be astoundingly generous, and somewhere in the course of the book might lend his wooden leg to another character for a night, as a splint for a broken limb. Or he might be amazingly forgetful, and often be met searching for the leg which he had just taken off for a moment.

Sometimes these minor characters become infused with sentiment. Although strange and unsuccessful in worldly terms, they are warmer and kinder than the principal characters around whom the story is built. Miss Tox seems originally to have been intended as just a sycophantic spinster friend of a domineering married woman, as someone whose social position suggested how necessary it was for women to marry. Yet she touches the reader's heart with her queer dignity after her 'friend' rebuffs and rebukes her. After that she acts on her own emotional impulses, in a warm-hearted and generous way. One impulse leads her back into the circle of warm fellowship that the good characters share; she starts to visit Polly Toodle and her family. She offers to make herself useful as a teacher to the children, if they will share their comfortable evenings with her. So life continues for the good, in a slowly increasing circle of affection while Mr Dombey and Mr Carker walk abroad in terrible solitude.

NOTES AND GLOSSARY:

acquirements:	accomplishments

Chapter 39: Further Adventures of Captain Edward Cuttle, Mariner

---

Rob leaves The Wooden Midshipman. The Captain opens Sol Gills's last packet, in the presence of his staunch friend Bunsby, and learns that Sol Gills had gone to the West Indies to look for Walter. Mrs Mac-Stinger suddenly appears. She is firmly escorted home by Bunsby, and even gives him the Captain's abandoned trunk.

COMMENTARY: Captain Cuttle's warm-hearted ruminations fill this chapter. He is deserted by Rob the Grinder, whom he understands sufficiently well to sense himself betrayed in his trust. The year from Gills's departure has now elapsed, so the Captain sends for Bunsby, and in his presence opens Gills's last letter. The letter reveals Gills's intention to search for Walter in the West Indies and mentions his wish that Walter, or if Walter is dead, the Captain, should succeed to his property. The Captain solemnly considers that he is the guardian, not the owner, of the little shop. But his peace of mind is severely ruffled as the MacStingers suddenly rush into his parlour. Mrs MacStinger attacks him in no kind spirit but the magnificent Bunsby quells her and leads her home. He returns, late at night, with the Captain's trunk. Then he departs and Captain Cuttle is left alone to reflect upon the new freedom he will enjoy as he waits for his lost friends to return.

NOTES AND GLOSSARY:
lachrymose: tearful

Chapter 40: Domestic Relations

The marriage of Mr and Mrs Dombey becomes more and more openly a mutual torment to them both. Dombey confronts Edith and she pleads with him to cease this warfare, to try to make their marriage work for Florence's sake.

COMMENTARY: Dombey seems almost to become a villain as he retreats into himself, and rejects Florence and Edith unless they first submit to him. Edith understands him, and refuses. Florence cannot even understand what he wants from her. She is in less spiritual danger than if she did; her yearning toward loving life will not be destroyed by losing itself in the dark cloudy castle of his thoughts, for she is not invited to dwell inside his life. She must look on from the outside.
Edith's appeal to Dombey is open, adult, and plainly spoken.

'You will further please, Madam,' said Mr Dombey, in a tone of sovereign command, 'to understand distinctly, that I am to be deferred to and obeyed. That I must have a positive show and confession of deference before the world, Madam. I am used to this. I require it as my right. In short I will have it. I consider it no unreasonable return for the worldly advancement that has befallen you; and I believe nobody will be surprised, either at its being returned from you, or at your making it. —To Me—To Me!—' he added with emphasis.

Edith stresses the loveless nature of their bargain, but offers him a truce, as between equal powers.

'I speak to you for the sake of others. Also your own sake; and for mine. Since our marriage, you have been arrogant to me; and I have repaid you in kind. You have shown to me and every one around us, every day and hour, that you think I am graced and distinguished by your alliance. I do not think so, and have shown that too. It seems you do not understand, or (so far as your power can go) intend that each of us shall take a separate course; and you expect from me instead, a homage you will never have.'

Although her face was still the same, there was emphatic confirmation of this 'Never' in the very breath she drew.

'I feel no tenderness towards you; that you know. You would care nothing for it, if I did or could. I know as well that you feel none towards me. But we are linked together; and in the knot that ties us, as I have said, others are bound up. We must both die; we are both connected with the dead already, each by a little child. Let us forbear.'

But he will have none of it. So any real hope ends for Edith Dombey. Through knowing Florence she has come to value love and to repent of marrying for money. She wants to try again, but Dombey's real villainy, his cruel freezing of hope in others, turns her cold again.

NOTES AND GLOSSARY:
asperity: sharpness of temper
temporise: to yield to the current of opinion

Chapter 41: New Voices in the Waves

Florence and Mr Toots revisit Blimper's Academy with tender feelings. Mrs Skewton dies, after several strokes.

COMMENTARY: This chapter relates the sorry death of Mrs Skewton. She is sent with Edith and Florence to Brighton, but Edith wishes to nurse her alone. The young woman sits with her mother night after night, trying to give her the comfort of a daughter's forgiveness and concern at her life's last hour. It would, however, take more than that forgiveness and concern to console Mrs Skewton for leaving the only life she wishes to have, the life of tolerable worldly amusements and of searching for ways to improve one's social position. Her friends shiver at her passing, and forget her. Even the gentle Florence shivers at such a death, though she peacefully visits the familiar places of young Paul's life in Brighton.

In this chapter the faithful Mr Toots secretly follows Florence to

Brighton. He then manages to encounter her and accompany her to Dr Blimper's Academy. After that visit, he proposes marriage to Florence, who, in a gentle and friendly way, discourages him.

NOTES AND GLOSSARY:
Lexicon: a dictionary

Chapter 42: Confidential and Accidental

Mr Dombey confers with Carker on private matters. Later he has an accident and chooses to recover under Mrs Pipchin's care, rather than his wife's.

COMMENTARY: Dombey turns to the evil Carker as a balm to his wounded pride. Carker's flattery is too persistent to be always misguided. Often it achieves its end, causing Dombey to reveal his weaknesses. Dombey requests Carker's service as an agent for Mrs Dombey's instruction. Carker will be the weapon in his hand as he humiliates Mrs Dombey into submission. But Carker is a willing agent, with evil designs on them all. His addresses to Mrs Dombey henceforth carry a suggestion of lust.

Dombey falls from his horse on the way home, and Carker brings his household the news of this mishap. Florence wishes to see her father, but Edith and Carker, from different motives, prevent her. Florence retains her innocence, but continues to suffer pointlessly.

NOTES AND GLOSSARY:
disapprobation: disapproval

Chapter 43: The Watches of the Night

Mr Dombey's illness brings to a head the conflict of emotions that makes his household a place of suffering.

COMMENTARY: Florence begins to sense that Edith and her father feel no love for each other. This realisation floods her sensitive soul with pain, as it marks the death of her hope for a real home life. She visits her father while he sleeps and gives him a kiss that is a gesture of farewell.

She returns upstairs to find Edith wild with tormented pride, and yet with a more dignified moral sorrow over her own confusions than she has ever shown. Edith has found the new experience of love both a steadying influence and a painful obligation. She would like to abandon herself to desperation and reckless action. But as she watches Florence fall into a troubled sleep, the first real friendship of Edith's life keeps her awake, steadfast in a night vigil.

NOTES AND GLOSSARY:
mollified: appeased, softened

Chapter 44: A Separation

Susan Nipper assails Mr Dombey for his neglect of Florence, and is dismissed.

COMMENTARY: The rising of Susan Nipper in a terrible and ferocious wrath breaks the early morning quiet at Dombey's house, with an unexpected flurry. She berates Mr Dombey severely, while he lies helpless in bed. Only the inopportune arrival of Mrs Pipchin, that sunken galleon of gentility who has risen again to menace the Dombey household, stops Susan speaking. Mrs Pipchin fires all her cannons: Susan is dismissed.

Weeping, Susan leaves the house with what dignity she can manage, and comforts herself that Mr Dombey may reflect uneasily on his neglect of Florence. Florence would know—and the reader knows—that he will only feel a sense of outrage. He has decided that Florence is unlikeable; those who love her, are in rebellion.

Mr Toots arrives in time to do a service to Susan. He escorts her to his own rooms, and gives her a meal, before carefully shepherding her to her coach. In parting, Susan thanks him so heartily that he blurts out his love for Florence, and Susan, ever honest, tells him that Florence could never think of him as a lover. Poor Toots can be left in no doubt, after her emphatic, sympathetic words.

NOTES AND GLOSSARY:
discomfiture: frustration, state of being overthrown
cabriolet: a light, one-horse, two-seater carriage
plasters: bandages

Chapter 45: The Trusty Agent

Carker taunts Edith with his growing power over her, but he himself succumbs to the inner tyranny of lust.

COMMENTARY: Mr Carker tempts poor Edith to make confidences to him in anger which she would never normally make. Then he tempts her to despair. The only good force in her life, her love for Florence, will ruin Florence, by attracting her father's revenge. Yet Edith's force and energy seem to equal Carker's; the reader is left wondering if he has properly calculated her strength.

Edith grows in stature through the book, because her life has been changed by the unexpected power of love. It is one thing to despise evil, and another to love innocence. Edith now finds both feelings at work.

Carker hopes to pervert her esteem for Florence into a new wave of self-loathing; he is a sadistic tormentor. The resourcefulness of Edith may yet foil him.

NOTES AND GLOSSARY:
audaciously: boldly
contumacy: obstinate disobedience
derogatory: detracting

Chapter 46: Recognizant and Reflective

Carker moves in like a stalking leopard. He intends Dombey's ruin. Meanwhile he himself is watched by Mrs Brown, who urges her daughter to revenge. She enlists the wavering services of Rob the Grinder.

COMMENTARY: This chapter belongs to the evil characters of the story. It opens with Carker searching Dombey's books, to learn the weaknesses of the firm. Then it passes on to Alice Brown and her mother, keeping watch on Carker, to learn his weaknesses, and preying upon Rob the Grinder. He has settled readily into the casual give and take of the criminal community. He can be squeezed for information about Carker. He will still manage to make his own crooked way, when others are allowing their cunning to be weakened and overwhelmed by passion.

Carker escapes lightly from the scrutiny of these people. It is the eyes of innocence which see his real hatred for Dombey, his pride which matches Dombey's own. He probes his brother's feelings about Dombey and is driven to betray his own. Carker believes all Dombey's clerks hate him as much as he does himself, but he is only sure of one person hating Dombey more. That is his unhappy wife, Edith, with whom Carker hopes to forge a dark union, to destroy Dombey's self-esteem.

NOTES AND GLOSSARY:
triton: in classical mythology, a sea demi-god
irascibility: proneness to anger

Chapter 47: The Thunderbolt

The unhappy marriage of Edith and Dombey drives both to desperation. Edith must also distance herself from Florence, lest Dombey take revenge on the girl.

COMMENTARY: Florence is utterly alone now, in a shadow-world of loves remembered, or hoped-for. Edith must refrain from spending time in her company, lest that attract her father's wrath. Susan is gone. Walter has disappeared, and Paul and her mother both call to her from beyond death. She begins to lose her hold on life, though not her sanity. It is a mark of the strength of character Dickens intends to demonstrate in Florence, that she does not seem to retreat from reality into the twilit, hopeless world of fantasy. She is protected partly by her youth, and partly by her virtue, her courage and firm purpose. She intends in some way to be useful in life. Frustration will give such a character an intensity of feeling, and acute powers of self-discipline and reflective patience. Florence feels deeper sympathy for those who suffer, as she begins inevitably to comprehend the weightiness of power, and the power of evil.

Edith Dombey suffers from that dark power in the two men who influence her fate. Carker has decided to humiliate Dombey; Edith is his most terrible weapon. Dombey flaunts his pride in storms of aggression. But he is defeated. Edith runs off with Carker in a midnight adventure born of mutual hatred for Dombey, and loathing of each other.

Florence's innocence is trampled down till it dies within her. When she tries to comfort her father with love, he strikes her, and orders her to leave. In a powerful gesture of self-assertion, Florence takes him at his word. She leave his house forever.

NOTES AND GLOSSARY:
refractory: stubborn and unmanageable

Chapter 48: The Flight of Florence

Florence goes to Sol Gills's shop, and there friends gather.

COMMENTARY: Dickens begins to draw his plot towards a harmonious conclusion. He brings together the characters whose sympathy for life will make them work together, and become a force for good.

Firstly Florence runs to Sol Gills's shop. There Captain Cuttle looks after her. Then, while she sleeps, Mr Toots arrives, bringing a message that someone awaits the Captain at a pub. When the Captain returns from the meeting, he is aglow with a strange happiness. The reader can only surmise that a loved one has returned. As a touch of pathos, Dickens adds the faithful dog Diogenes to the company around Florence. Susan, too, is brought to mind. This chapter is a rallying point.

The characters gathering here are wiser and stronger than they used to be. They have acquired a certain dignity peculiar to Dickens's good characters: eccentricity remains, fragility is gone. A persistent goodness of nature strengthens them. Their characters settle into a quiet resolution; they will protect Florence in order to allow her to begin a serious adult life. She responds in her turn, and undertakes adult responsibility.

This scene, so characteristically Dickensian in its oddity, is also true to the author's deeper perception, that goodness must be serious, and strong, if it is to continue to survive in the world.

NOTES AND GLOSSARY:
adjuration: act of solemnly charging one with a duty
pertinacious: stubborn

Chapter 49: The Midshipman Makes a Discovery

In this chapter Florence's dearest friend Walter is restored to her. He has survived the shipwreck and returned home.

COMMENTARY: Florence has reached her harbour, and realises it. The peace she feels is shaken by sorrow, but she has a new dignity, because rather than be utterly despised, she asserted herself, and went out alone to those who would value her. She is a woman now, making plans for her own life. Dickens has created in Florence a gentlewoman who is strong as well as tender and generous. The traditional Victorian woman of Florence's class is seen here—as in other Victorian novels such as Mrs Gaskell's *Wives and Daughters* or George Eliot's *Middlemarch*—to be capable of immense influence on other people's lives, though her own life remains private. Although she has deserted wealth and power by leaving her father's house, Florence will seem significant to her friends. She is a foil to Edith, who lost the real power of womanhood by seeking to unite herself to wealth and power through a mercenary marriage. In Dickens's view, a woman is a moral force for good or ill; she rules the world's heart. The best male characters are those devoted to a good woman.

Joy suddenly breaks into Florence's life. Walter Gay returns to the small shop he loves. His story is related to Florence: shipwreck; bravery and survival; eventual return home. Dombey would wince to see them together, in the bloom of their youth, united by a natural sympathy. Captain Cuttle rejoices to see an old dream revived. And Walter, now a young man, begins to want this dream to become reality.

NOTES AND GLOSSARY:
sonorous: resonant, with a rich tone

Chapter 50: Mr Toots's Complaint

Walter asks Florence to marry him and is accepted joyfully. Susan is going to be reunited with the group by the efforts of Mr Toots.

COMMENTARY: In this chapter Florence finds the real work of her womanhood. She will be Walter's wife. The breath of romance has been dispelled by sorrow and poverty, but something simple and plainly loving exists between them. Loyalty, so deep as to bode well for the long voyage of life, will make them travel together; from now on their adventures will be shared. Walter will make his way in the world strengthened by pride in providing for her; she will make a home of wherever they find themselves. There is a moral equality between them. The truth to life of the Victorians' view of marriage exists in their deep sense of the need for that moral equality in a good marriage. Working at home, or outside the home, is not really the significant issue in marriage. Mutual respect, mutual cherishing, committed vigour make the Victorian characters come alive in their love for each other.

NOTES AND GLOSSARY:
abaft: behind

Chapter 51: Mr Dombey and the World

This chapter gives a brief description of the social world in which Dombey moves, offering its sympathy to him.

COMMENTARY: This chapter is almost comic. Mr Dombey's proud sins may isolate him from everyone but the world busies itself around him with a show of flustered feelings. He is called upon by Cousin Feenix, who suggests divorce, and by Joe Bagstock, who calls for a duel between Dombey and the offending Carker. Miss Tox calls secretly, disguised as a servant. She genuinely feels for his sorrow, and regrets his suffering, but she is not bold enough to offer him consolation. Like small rocks orbiting his dusty moon, these companions move in Dombey's chilly white light. He does not mention Florence to any of them. Even his sister, daring enough to mention her name, is cut so short that she can only hope Dombey does not believe she was confessing to harbouring Florence!

A world away from them all, Florence moves on as she wishes to move, no longer influenced by her father's whims.

NOTES AND GLOSSARY:
inculpated: involved in guilt

Chapter 52: Secret Intelligence

Dombey begins to track down Edith and Carker.

COMMENTARY: Low life bustles around Mr Dombey now, as he bends his will toward finding those who have offended his pride. Rob the

Grinder knows the whereabouts of Carker and Edith, but the secret is locked in his greasy soul until fear turns the key. That key is turned by old Mrs Brown, who has reared Rob as much in crime as Dombey has encouraged him to chase money. How well he has learned these lessons! He breaks faith with Carker and tells Mrs Brown that the unhappy pair are to meet at Dijon in France. No scruple troubles him, or her, as she allows Dombey to overhear this conversation, knowing murder may be the outcome. She counts her money and rejoices.

This is crime's end, as Dickens sees it. Fear, blackmail, and greed are so consuming that the criminal's personality quivers in the balance, shivering toward madness. The violence of crime consists of, in the first place, an assault on the persons of its victims, reducing the criminal's vision of them to a pocket to rob, or a body to rape. In the second place, it reduces the doer to a hand that robs, or a body that assaults. Both victim and doer thus suffer degradation. Dickens sees this with a piercing clarity; such figures stand out in his novels with an almost comic grotesquerie. But his final vision of crime is not comic.

NOTES AND GLOSSARY:
lachrymose: tearful

Chapter 53: More Intelligence

In this chapter events swiftly follow each other. Mr Dombey is bent on revenge, but Alice Brown's feelings are in a turmoil. She helps him to discover where his wife and Carker are, then repents and turns to Harriet Carker for help. Dombey's firm begins to collapse.

COMMENTARY: Mr Dombey's world is in ruins. He is thirsty for revenge. His first target is Carker's brother John, whom he summarily dismisses. Mr Morfin, Harriet's friend, arrives at the house of John and Harriet Carker, to solace them. Morfin speaks of himself as usually guilty of the habit of nine-tenths of the world of believing that all about him is right because he is used to it, but he shows himself deeply stirred by their misfortunes. He tells Harriet privately that though the firm will not go down under the cloud of dishonesty, it may well go down, through ill-considered ventures that come to little or nothing. Carker has pampered and deceived Dombey, and then left him to face complete ruin. Harriet has much to worry her as she sits by her fireside that evening, but she is disturbed by a face at her window that is no mere spirit. Alice Brown has come to tell her more about her brother's sins. He ruined her. In revenge, she has forced Rob to tell, in Dombey's hearing, where James Carker is hiding with Edith. Alice seems almost like a spirit, too troubled for death, as she tells Harriet to find James and warn him of Dombey's approach. Dickens mixes the natural with the supernatural throughout the chapter. Though Harriet is innocent, her mind will be played with and haunted by the spirits of evil among which she has lived. Though valiant, she may well quail as she attempts to rescue her brother.

NOTES AND GLOSSARY:
wainscot partition: thin wall of wood panels

Chapter 54: The Fugitives

Carker and Edith meet in Dijon, but Edith rejects his advances. She feels terror, but breaks past him and flees. English people are near them, and Carker flees as well.

COMMENTARY: Decadence mingles with decay in the French apartment where Edith Dombey and James Carker speak to each other, after bringing the man they both hate to desperation. The false communion of an elaborate supper is prepared for them. But Edith takes only a knife from the table, a knife with which to murder Carker if he approaches her. His terrible lust is seen for what it is—he would make her lost soul his own, in a hellish mating. There is knocking at the hall door. English voices, bent on vengeance, pursue them as Edith defies him. Edith leaves the room and Carker cannot find her. Eventually he finds a second way out of the apartment, and begins his terrible flight.

Here Dickens reveals again that in crime there is no friendship, only a terrible bond of mutual hate and mistrust. Life offers Edith little now, but she has made one last attempt to redeem herself from the evil in which she has long been enmeshed. She goes alone into the night.

James Carker, too, is alone, but he is making no last stand. Only a flight into nothingness, close to madness, can take him from this place. All human relationship is ending for him, who planned to master life, seizing it on his own terms, whatever the cost to others. For the sadist with no one left to torture, there is only the dark.

NOTES AND GLOSSARY:
odious: hateful
pinion: to cut off the wings of a bird so that it cannot fly; to confine by binding the arms

Chapter 55: Rob the Grinder Loses his Place

This awesome chapter tells of Carker's last journey and death.

COMMENTARY: Carker decides to return to England. In the shadowy streets, in the middle of the night, he takes a coach whose driver could be Death himself, yet the desperate Carker asks him for all speed:

Hallo! Hi! away at a gallop over the black landscape, dust and dirt flying like spray, the smoking horses snorting and plunging as if each of them were ridden by a demon, away in a frantic triumph on the dark road—whither?

The open countryside at daybreak brings Carker's mind no rest. He is at war with himself, for having been deceived by Edith and nearly entrapped by Dombey. Like every villain, he has believed himself the centre of his miserable stage, the cleverest person walking on it. But he has been despised by one he thought to master, and his broken pride makes a coward of him. Dickens is never without pity; the reader senses here a human being struggling with dark and terrible passions, losing all grip on himself. Terror and pity stir in the reader, the old emotions a tragic hero can evoke are stirred for a man losing his soul.

Carker travels back to England, pursued by Dombey. He has vague ideas about returning to a place in the country that he knows, but the real shadow of Death is overtaking him with every stage of his journey. When he reaches a railway station, he reaches doom. Like vengeance, the train slaughters him, fire and darkness overwhelming what was once a man. But, even for Carker, Dickens reminds the reader, there may be a last moment of remorse and a flash of new beginning.

> . . . he turned to where the sun was rising, and beheld it, in its glory, as it broke upon the scene.
>
> So awful, so transcendent in its beauty, so divinely solemn. As he cast his faded eyes upon it, where it rose, tranquil and serene, unmoved by all the wrong and wickedness on which its beams had shone since the beginning of the world, who shall say that some weak sense of virtue upon earth, and its reward in Heaven, did not manifest itself, even to him? If ever he remembered sister or brother with a touch of tenderness and remorse, who shall say it was not then?

NOTES AND GLOSSARY:
suffusion: overspreading, as with a liquid, tinge, or tint

Chapter 56: Several People Delighted, and the Game Chicken Disgusted

---

The company of friends assemble at the old instrument-maker's shop. Sol Gills returns.

COMMENTARY: Susan rejoins Florence at The Midshipman, rejoicing with her about her intended marriage, and grieving wildly over her distressed circumstances. Mr Toots is full of misery but takes comfort from Susan. He is alarmed to hear that Florence will sail to China with Walter, but Captain Cuttle, that veteran dreamer, assures him all will be well. Polly, too, is brought again in to the circle of friends. A sharp contrast between the warm companionship of the good friends and the terrible aloneness of Carker's death comes to the reader's mind. So Florence, meek and gentle, becomes the centre of a circle of love at the very time when the world could scorn her. But one friend is missing. Young Paul Dombey comes often into Florence's mind, and she shares her sorrow with Walter.

One last great joy comes the way of the party at the instrument-maker's shop. The evening before Florence is to marry Walter, the shop-owner returns, to the wonderment of them all. Sol Gills tells them he wrote many letters to poor Captain Cuttle whose flight from his landlady meant he never received one. But in the joy of reunion, old sorrows are quickly overtaken by new hopes.

NOTES AND GLOSSARY:
dishevelled: disordered, disarranged

Chapter 57: Another Wedding

Florence and Walter are quietly married and set off for China. Walter leaves a note for Mr Dombey. Captain Cuttle is comforted by Sol Gills, and Mr Toots by Susan.

COMMENTARY: Love opens new horizons in this chapter, and new adventures are begun. Florence and Walter include all their friends in their happiness, even young Paul, whose grave they visit on their wedding day. The sea that they travel will always speak to Florence of Paul's belief in life after death, and his longing to go to a real home where love is the order of being, the very nature of its reality. In that shared confidence she unashamedly unites her sorrows to her joy. Walter loves her deeply, as Paul did. She gives to him the earnest loyalty and steadfast encouragement she gave to her brother. When younger, she had called Walter her brother, but now as a woman she experiences a new depth of love, and takes her rightful place as the welcome warmth and light in her husband's life.

All the friends share the wedding day festivity. They weep, and laugh. They say their goodbyes and comfort one another. Theirs is a continuing pledge of mutual support and affection that always looks toward tomorrow, with hope.

NOTES AND GLOSSARY:
beadle: an official attendant who walks before dignitaries, often a mace-bearer (the word can also mean a parish officer, a church, or court officer)

Chapter 58: After a Lapse

Dombey's firm collapses into ruin. Harriet Carker's goodness is made obvious. Alice Brown dies, in her care.

COMMENTARY: As the world chatters angrily about bad debts, the House of Dombey is declared bankrupt. Dombey himself retires, a broken man whose total solitude can be seen to be the inevitable consequence of pride; he is lost to the touch of human sympathy. Harriet Carker and her good brother try to bridge the moat Dombey's pride has made around him, but respect his final choice, giving him help anonymously through Mr Morfin. Harriet's care extends also to Alice Brown, who lies wasting in sickness. Harriet visits her nightly, and pays for nursing care. Dickens connects Alice to Edith Dombey again in the reader's mind. Often before, they have seemed parallel figures; now it is revealed they are first cousins, though Alice's birth was illegitimate. Harriet reads to Alice from the Gospel, of which Dickens says they

> read the eternal book for all the weary and the heavy-laden, for all the wretched, fallen, and neglected of this earth—read the blessed history, in which the blind lame palsied beggar, the criminal, the woman stained with shame, the shunned of all our dainty clay, has each a portion that no human pride, indifference, or sophistry, through all the ages that this world shall last, can take away, or by the thousandth atom of a grain reduce—read the ministry of Him who, through the round of human life and all its hopes and griefs, from birth to death, from infancy to age, had sweet compassion for, and interest in, its every scene and stage, its every suffering and sorrow.

This is Dickens's deeply held conviction. What to a modern reader may seem naively overt, seemed heartfelt to a Victorian. Dickens believed in Christianity's teaching that the despised and the admired are equally cared for by God, and that special compassion reaches to those who are fallen, but long to stand up again. Dickens cherished innocence, but he also deeply believed in forgiveness.

NOTES AND GLOSSARY:
inducement: lure

Chapter 59: Retribution

Dombey is ruined and filled with remorse. He longs to see Florence. One day she returns, telling him she has a child. He accepts her love with gratitude and joy.

COMMENTARY: The Dombey house is stripped of its furniture, which is sold off. The servants seek other places, and the gentle-minded Miss Tox can only weep for the fate of her hero. Dombey keeps to his room brooding on his past, and longing for Florence.

Dickens believed in the Christian Gospel which tells of the redemption even of the most unloving heart. Dombey suffers, but that suffering prepares the ground for the possibility of the growth of real love. When Florence returns Dombey longs to see her, and to tell her that she is welcome as his daughter, though he feels utterly unworthy of her. When she does come he is filled with delight and they are reconciled. She needs his love, and he gives it joyfully.

NOTES AND GLOSSARY:

gigs: a gig is a light, two-wheeled, one-horse carriage

Chapter 60: Chiefly Matrimonial

This chapter relates that Mr Toots has married Susan Nipper, to their mutual joy. Old acquaintances are also spoken of: Mr Feeder marries Cornelia Blimper, and Mrs MacStinger marries Bunsby.

COMMENTARY: Marriage is the theme of this chapter: Mr Feeder, B.A., is to marry Cornelia Blimper, and Mr Toots has brought to the wedding his own wife, Susan Nipper. Feeder and Toots agree about the joys of marriage:

'You see,' said Mr Toots, 'what *I* wanted in a wife was—in short, was sense. Money, Feeder, I had. Sense I—I had not, particularly.'

When Mr and Mrs Toots return to their hotel they find a letter awaiting them. This announces the amazing news that Dombey is reconciled with Florence and that Florence is caring for him in her own home.

Captain Cuttle's pleasure in the recent wedding of Toots and Susan, and his joy in Florence's baby, is only overshadowed by the bizarre triumph of Mrs MacStinger, in leading poor Bunsby to the altar. After the bleak wedding feast, the Captain goes on to Florence's. Mr and Mrs Toots are already there, and the happy reunion between Florence and Susan is a warm pleasure to all.

NOTES AND GLOSSARY:

Hymen: The Greek god of marriage

Chapter 61: Relenting

Dombey is desperately ill, but he is happy with Florence. Edith Dombey has a last visit from Florence; she too is altered and she wants Florence to know of her repentance.

COMMENTARY: Dombey is ill and weak, and is cared for by Florence and Susan. Cousin Feenix takes Florence to Edith. It is a passionately sad meeting, for Florence is the only person ever to break through Edith's pride, to reach her heart. Edith has written down the truth about the events in France, and presents it to Florence to give to Dombey if she thinks it right. Edith has repented and believes Dombey too will repent, through learning to care for Florence.

NOTES AND GLOSSARY:
conjunctions: alignments with or coincidences with

Chapter 62: Final

The Madeira wine is finally opened and a convivial gathering enjoys it. Mr Dombey is included, as Sol Gills and the Captain celebrate Walter's return, his marriage to Florence, and the birth of his son. This last chapter is full of hope. Seemingly endless sorrows and sufferings are ended, and a new sense of adventure is in the air. The deep friendships among Captain Cuttle, Sol Gills, Walter, Susan, Mr Toots, and Florence start to bring sunlight and warmth even to Mr Dombey. Life begins to renew them all. Like the last act of a Shakespearean comedy, Dickens's novel ends amidst weddings. Susan Nipper is married to Mr Toots, and they have a family of three little girls. Harriet Carker marries Mr Morfin and they settle happily with her brother. Dickens tells his readers that Florence and Walter have two children, whom Mr Dombey loves dearly. A sweet peace settles over all their lives, a sense of everyday harmonies that give dignity to loss, redemption to evil, and hope to all the living.

NOTES AND GLOSSARY:
loquacious: talkative
connubial: married

Part 3

Commentary

Dombey and Son is a vivid social novel, as well as a gripping story about a young girl growing up among extraordinary trials. The reader is being asked to think about the capitalist values to which Dombey subscribes in the light of older, more genuine values of family life and friendship. The unexpected resourcefulness of human beings, and their capacity for steadfast caring warm a book which tells of so much unhappiness. Human relationships are endangered by being seen as contracts, (just or unjust), but survive as nurturing bonds. The new social order is seen as no threat so long as it allows the older mutual supportiveness to continue.

Themes

Dombey and Son has several themes, some negative, some positive. Like many of Dickens's books, it can be read by children or adults of different ages and viewed differently in the light of their experiences. Florence, the book's central character, begins the story as a young child whose anguish Dickens almost seems to share; she matures throughout the book to young womanhood, keeping the same circle of friends, but gradually changing her relationships with them.

The vanity of the world

Some of the book's minor characters are deeply enmeshed in the worldly traffic of reputations. Joe Bagstock even forgets his peevishness at Dombey's rivalry for Miss Tox's esteem, in his wish to take advantage of Dombey's regard to enhance himself as a 'man of the world'. He introduces Dombey to Mrs Skewton and her unhappy daughter Edith Granger, who will cause Dombey much misery while they are married. All four share a view of marriage as a contract of mutual worldly advantage with almost no real basis of mutual affection. Edith, having a deeper, less mercenary nature, cannot keep that contract; her real feelings break through both in her sullen refusal to help Dombey in any way, and in her sudden discovery of real love for Florence. Like Joe Bagstock, Mrs Skewton exists by playing a character whose repertoire is limited. Edith breaks through this play-acting a little when her mother is dying, as she alternately accuses her mother and tends to her lovingly. If so, it is a partial redemption.

Edith also begs Dombey to reconsider using the world as a looking-glass for his vanity, and to try to re-establish his marriage on a different footing, but

> 'You will further please, Madam,' said Mr Dombey in a tone of sovereign command, 'to understand distinctly that I am to be deferred to and obeyed. That I must have a positive show and confession of deference before the world, Madam.' (Chapter 40)

After this, Edith's chief moral struggle will be to forgive him, not to be reconciled with him.

The low esteem in which Mr Carker the Manager holds his brother and sister is an intense version of the hate and fear with which failure is met in the world. But their true value is sensed by Mr Morfin who, despite the dulling habit of accepting life as it is without question, breaks out of a conventional placidity to seek them out and offer help.

The dignity of women

From the introduction of Susan Nipper and Polly Toodle in the early chapters Dickens starts a theme he will explore throughout the book. He will emphasise again and again that women have tremendous inner resources of courageous love. It is this trait which to some extent at least saves Edith Dombey and Alice Brown from the destructive anger in themselves. Florence grows up knowing the goodness in other women and this, along with the help and care given to her by Captain Cuttle and her faith in Walter, sustains her through bleak months. As a girl she is able to be a mainstay to young Paul, and as a woman she will steady and encourage Walter. She does this, however, after facing the possibility of life without him, an experience which adds a freely felt joy to her love for Walter.

Three of the women partly assert their dignity through marrying, although they cannot bring their husbands worldly advantage: Harriet Carker marries Mr Morfin; Susan Nipper marries Mr Toots; and Florence marries Walter Gay. They provide good judgment and initiative, courage beyond the normal in being so steadfast. Again and again their innate dignity is asserted.

The isolation of pride

Mr Dombey insulates himself from life in his terrible pride. He trusts his flatterers, Mr Carker and Joe Bagstock, but eventually suffers in marriage and even in business by listening to the wrong people, and totally ignoring what others say. His pride is symbolised by his big house, most of which is empty. He lives in a small area downstairs and Edith and Florence live in separate rooms upstairs. Dickens suggests that Dombey suffers in this self-inflicted isolation. He is always a human being trapped inside himself, and thus Dickens makes his slow recovery believable.

Carker's sexual pride is overweening and cruel, as is his pride in his business ability. He is filled with resentment and longs for power. Although Dickens does not finally damn him, he dies alone.

Alice Brown, like Edith Granger, feels she has been abused, that her spirit has been tormented, but not broken. But both these women learn to forgive, and, in doing so, earn the respect of others.

Journeys

One of the *motifs* or recurring images in *Dombey and Son* is the journey. Young Florence and Paul journey to Brighton to school, and the bond between them grows deeper. Later, Florence's visit to the Skettleses takes place at the time when she is growing to womanhood, accepting her suffering without blaming herself. Her brief trips to The Wooden Midshipman lead eventually to her making a new home there.

Walter's long, dangerous sea voyage only increases the value others see in him, and ends in a happy return. When he must travel again, Florence will go with him.

Sol Gill's search for Walter is paralleled in loyalty by the short, risky journey Captain Cuttle makes, moving from Mrs MacStinger's to the shop, to keep a home waiting for the travellers.

Dombey's trip with Major Bagstock, however, is fraught with danger to his pride. He resents the way in which the Toodles mourn for Paul. He drinks in the flattery of Joe Bagstock and Carker, and deceives himself into thinking that marriage to Edith will bring them both mutual gratification. By comparison, even Alice Brown's journey brings some reward.

The most terrible journey of the book is the flight of Edith and Carker. This is a nightmare of pursuit and hostility. Dickens captures the fear felt by Carker and the desperate bravery shown by Edith. In their journeys the characters reveal their inner selves, and the outer landscape merely serves as a backdrop to this revelation.

Plot and structure

The plot of *Dombey and Son* is more carefully made than that of some of Dickens's other novels. There are fewer jerks in the action and fewer uses of coincidence. One of the few really startling coincidences in the book is Alice Brown's seduction by James Carker. Yet Dickens makes such full use of this in the plot that the reader is willing to suspend disbelief. Alice plays a decisive part in the story, and is not merely a minor character. She exacts revenge, but then she repents and tries to save Carker. This brings her into contact with Harriet Carker again. They become close, and Harriet nurses Alice through her last illness.

In general, this novel is remarkable for the development of minor characters into almost major characters, whose crises are as real to the reader as those of Edith, Florence, or Dombey. The happy and the unhappy mix as in real life. Florence's relationship with Walter is strengthened by his comprehension of her grief over Paul. Walter also understands her wish to be reconciled with her father, and her grief over Edith's sad life and failures. Florence must get along with only limited emotional support from her stepmother, but she manages.

The action of the novel connects the characters closely by making them know each other under different circumstances. Carker is Dombey's manager, Edith's tormentor, Walter's boss, brother to John and Harriet Carker, and seducer of Alice Brown. Individual stories, like those of Alice and Edith, link in this way. A minor character such as Miss Tox can appear and reappear, first in Dombey's household, later on her own, and then later in the Toodle household. This enables Dickens to express one of the book's main themes: that the good in people surfaces despite the odds. It demonstrates the variety of experience within a life.

Settings

Dickens uses settings to create vivid impressions of the characters' lives. He places his characters in settings that are almost *caricatures* or cartoons in their simplicity and animation. The Wooden Midshipman, for example, reflects the people who live there or come there in its orderliness, its unassuming dignity that makes no demands on customers to buy. This atmosphere, in turn, influences the characters, calming Captain Cuttle and Florence. A great contrast to it is Mrs Pipchin's boarding house, so much an 'establishment', so little a home. Details build up the impression that her own comforts are catered for, but no one else's.

Dr Blimper's academy is a place where knowledge is exalted above all else. Dickens feels strongly about the pumping of facts into children, and makes the process seem both comical and grotesque. He redeems it somewhat by showing that there is a general, if limited, kindliness to Paul, and by carrying on the story of Mr Toots even to his eventual return to attend the wedding of the tutor, Mr Feeder, and the young lady of the house, Cornelia Blimper.

Near both Dr Blimper's academy and Mrs Pipchin's is the sea, where Paul goes to wonder 'what the waves are always saying'. Throughout the story the sea is a powerful image of life after death calling to the living.

Dombey's house is a place where things lie unused except in a few rooms where Dombey, Susan and Florence, and Edith live. When the house is redecorated after Dombey's second marriage, nothing changes. It does not come to life. Edith denies Dombey the pleasure of having her as hostess at dinner parties, and so not even formal social functions are held there.

Dickens and Victorian melodrama

Dickens loved the Victorian theatre, although he was dissatisfied with stage adaptations of his own writings. He liked amateur dramatics, puppet shows, and dramatic public readings. The Victorians gave colourful performances of Shakespeare, but the staple of their theatre productions was melodrama, a form of play in which good and evil characters battle through many crises over the fate of the innocent. Almost always the good triumphs and the innocent are rescued, remaining innocent, but not necessarily becoming wiser. The influence of these plays on Dickens's writing is marked. His central, good characters are often children or young women, who pass through terrible, morally-threatening dangers and remain true to their ideals even when they themselves are misunderstood and perhaps rejected. These characters are often given great support by rather grotesque, good-hearted people, who never achieve worldly success in the unequal struggle of life. Because of their own failures, these characters are often strangely clear-sighted and help the central characters when more prosperous, more settled people abandon them.

From his involvement with theatre Dickens also took a strong sense of crucial scenes which linger in a reader's imagination. Setting is almost metaphoric for Dickens, as it is in melodrama, or in children's fairy tales. Blimper's Academy is a good example of such a place. It represents a grinding world of achievement that Paul cannot hope to enter. When he lies very ill in the midst of the school party, the best relationship of that world seems to him to be summed up in the affectionate pity bestowed on him by the moving figures who notice him quietly observing the scene. Another major scene is that of Florence's confrontation with her father which leads to her flight from home; this is very melodramatic. She is struck but not badly hurt, and the relationship between love offered and love rejected is clearly defined. The offer must, for a time, be withdrawn. But Dickens is anxious to provide a happy ending, and so the weaker scene of her reunion with a repentant

Dombey must be staged. Innocent good can then achieve its own humble triumph.

The characters

Florence

Florence Dombey is one of Dickens's strong female characters. Her courage is supported by her ability to trust other people. She mothers Paul, but she herself turns first to Susan, and then to Walter, and later to Walter's friend the captain. She is wise enough to sense her own weakness.

She is a character which grows in the course of the novel. From the early, motherly figure, she matures into someone who learns to live with sorrow and rejection. She comes to see herself not just as Paul's sister and, later, as Walter's wife, but as a member of a circle of mutually helpful friends. Her resolve to live when she believes Walter is dead is a mark of her strength. She comes to realise that evil and madness exist without being daunted by this realisation. A reader feels that she will give Walter the support of her wisdom, without his fully understanding her mind.

Walter

For Walter Gay, life is an adventure which must be tackled. He is enthusiastic and ever hopeful. His affections run deep, but his love is really based on respect and affection rather than the absorbing seriousness of passion. He is not as courageous as his friends because he seldom experiences fear. But they love his boyish companionship, which has its own resilience. Making light of difficulties is indeed often a step toward overcoming them. Walter is a simpler character than Florence but immensely steadfast. Unlike her deep feeling, his sunny courage is almost a physical quality. Defeat is something Walter could walk away from, to try again something else, but the drive toward reconciliation and toward redeeming the past belongs to Florence alone. Walter is an achiever who will give Florence the material comfort she might never seek. He is manly in his urge to provide for her, and to protect her and his other friends. He is perpetually likeable, and, like Florence, has great strength of purpose.

Carker

Carker is a deeply interesting character, somewhat like Iago in Shakespeare's *Othello*. His jealousy of Dombey hides behind the obsequious service he offers him, but he is psychologically astute enough to feed Dombey's undermining fault, pride. Under this dark tutelage, Dombey falls deeper and deeper into the horrifying isolation of pride, imagining himself to be the centre of an admiring circle, a sharp contrast to Florence, who really is such a centre. Carker is subtle and sadistic, an astute reader of other people's weaknesses. But he remains blind to his own, which is also pride, sexual pride. When he realises this, the knowledge drives him to suicidal madness. He is a character whom a reader learns to pity, a fact which is a measure of Dickens's achievement in creating depth in the characters of *Dombey and Son*.

John Carker and Harriet Carker

These people are the foil to others' achievements, for they must live out their lives in failure, and they remain overshadowed. Harriet marries late, and is childless; John will never make his mark in the outside world. While John Carker blames himself excessively for an early misdemeanour and Harriet carries loyalty almost to a cloying sweetness, they are an authentic part of the shadowy world of Victorian business, in which many lives were wrecked. Their presence reflects Dickens's realism, and indicates that some of the damage evil does cannot be quite undone. Young lives are more easily redeemed than older ones, which sometimes live with hardship, enduring more than seems fair. Justice is elusive for Dickens, despite the book's happy ending. The Carkers become friends of Florence and Walter only as the story ends, but that does not prevent John being an influence on young Walter's life earlier; perhaps they influence each other crucially, for he teaches Walter the reality of sorrow, and Walter teaches him hope. Harriet's compassion for Alice Brown and later for Edith Dombey comes partly out of her own acceptance of sorrow. She is one to watch over the dying, and give them dignity. But she is also a friend whose love can be joyous, as it is when she marries Mr Morfin.

Paul

Paul Dombey is a child whose life has scarcely begun. He is isolated from the world by his own terrible need for his father's approval. When his father can sanction neither Paul's love for Florence, nor his affection and respect for his humbler friends, Paul knows he cannot live. But he goes on doing his best to do so. Many people become fond of him and he of them. He is generous and enthusiastic about Florence's life. He is unaware of the sorrow she feels for him, because he trusts her to help him to live.

Mr Dombey

Mr Dombey's character is cold and puzzling for most of the story. But his final redemption is more substantial than mere sentimentality, for throughout the book deep repressed feelings have rippled the surface of Dombey's life. He is someone who can scarcely love. In the end, Florence's acceptance of him and her continued desire for his love break through his defences. Dombey's pride falls, his public position disappears, and he begins to live a private life. His loss of occupation is a drastic piece of surgery but he finds that he is able to care for Florence's son as much as he did for Paul.

Edith

Edith is a deeply troubled woman, whose frustration and anger almost destroy her. Her scorn for herself is her own deepest emotion, and yet the worst thing that she does, running off with Carker, is her strongest assertion that she does have dignity. In no other positive way can she affirm her identity. She feels trapped and cornered by society. She is very tender toward Florence, and that loving bond brings the steadying refusal to commit adultery with Carker. In the closing chapters Edith, like Alice Brown, is in a twilight between living and dying.

Captain Cuttle and Sol Gills

These lovable eccentrics are the mainstay of Walter's young life, giving him a wholesome start in the art of friendship that enables him to win Florence. They are incurably hopeful people whom life treats as it will, without damaging their fundamental good nature and warm-heartedness. They lack refinement but have the real good manners born of a general willingness to value goodness wherever they meet it, and an immense capacity for loyalty. Their strength supports Florence through her troubles. They are as steadfast as the evening star, and take their bearings from a general unselfishness that makes them encourage the young people through every difficulty. Want of money is no real obstacle to a happiness built on human relationships and a passionate zest for the adventure of living. Around them the instruments of science shine, without dampening their view that life is a seaman's story, full of conquered misfortune, and with a moral message.

Susan Nipper

The sharp-tongued young woman with a heart of gold is Florence's chief companion in dark years. Despised by the household god Mr

Dombey, but loved by Florence and Paul, Susan keeps her own opinions well-aired and fresh. She, too, is immensely loyal, a trait Dickens greatly values, and gives to his best characters in many novels. (Indeed, *Great Expectations* could be said to be about a young man learning to be loyal despite his faults.) Susan keeps Florence sane by speaking out against the evils about her. Her refusal to be impressed by what the world admires gives her courage, and it is courage she teaches to Florence, whose gentleness must be tempered like steel if she is to survive.

Mr Morfin

Mr Morfin has a quiet goodness that waits to be stirred to gentle action. He is a creature of habit and instinct, like a wild rabbit. He is deeply disturbed by discovering the truth about the three Carkers, and makes a new habit of visiting Harriet and John. Although he is almost an eccentric, Dickens gives him an ability to grow out of his retiring habits, and eventually to marry.

Major Bagstock

J.B. Bagstock is a fair-weather friend who attaches himself to Dombey, hoping to share the prestige and seeming pleasures of Dombey's life. He is indifferent to everyone but himself. He also suggests England's cruelly unfeeling attitude to her colonies in his surliness toward the coloured servant on whom he depends. His chief love is comfort, and he is his own greatest audience.

Lucretia Tox and Mr and Mrs Chick

Miss Tox is a good-hearted lady whose real affections are somewhat concealed behind her anxious desire to please people. She really admires Dombey for his achievements and his energy; she is very fond of young Paul, and very kindly. She is accepted by the Toodles and there her own warm heart finds a family to care for.

The Chicks are destined never to understand each other. Mrs Chick, Dombey's sister, is not ruthless, although she has her share of pride. Mr Chick continues his good-hearted, puzzled way through life despite his wife's ups and downs, her exaltations and her resentments. Mrs Chick at first encourages Lucretia Tox's feeling for Dombey, then drops her after Dombey remarries. She too longs for Dombey's approval, and sacrifices her friendship for Miss Tox to gain it. Dombey is almost indifferent to her, although he does sometimes ask for her advice.

Polly

Warm-hearted affection radiates from Polly, who originally takes a job looking after Paul to help her own growing family, and she has to change her name and pretend indifference to them to help to support them. But her warmth soon makes a bond between herself and Paul, and she is one of the people he wants to see when he is dying.

Polly also befriends Florence and, with some difficulty, Susan Nipper. Her family will rise throughout the book, benefiting from the new railway line, with the exception of her eldest boy, 'Biler'. He is corrupted by bad education, arranged by Mr Dombey, and is then influenced by Carker.

Dickens's achievement in *Dombey and Son*

Dombey and Son is a long, complex novel with many characters, but Dickens manages this intricate structure successfully by using sub-plots which vary the action and show the many characters in different situations. As the plots interconnect we see many strengths and weaknesses in a character. Captain Cuttle, inarticulate but warm, gives great comfort and support to Walter, and later to Florence, but is deceived and badly treated by Rob ('Biler') and James Carker. Polly is seen at home, as well as in the awkward role she has to fill at work. She is shown making friends wherever she goes and trying to help her eldest son. Miss Tox moves innocently and sincerely in a range of relationships, unaware that Joe Bagstock makes fun of her to Dombey, belittling her when he realises that she prefers Dombey to him. This gives the book depth, and unity. *Dombey and Son* can, then, develop great themes, such as the need for human affection, and the possible redemption of people who have done evil.

Dombey and Son is a novel about the inner feelings and distress of its characters and it is these that give the book great strength, making a lasting impression on the reader. Although Dickens's crystal-clear impressions of characters give the book the symbolic, almost magical quality of much of his other writing, it is closer in tone to later Victorian novels such as George Eliot's *Middlemarch* (1871–2). The social background remains simply the backdrop and not the all-pervasive influence it becomes in Dickens's *Bleak House* (1852–3). In that respect, *Dombey and Son* foreshadows his next book *David Copperfield* (1849–50).

This book does, however, take up one social theme, the importance of women to one and all, to children, to men, and to other girls and women. The sad stories of Edith Granger Dombey and of Alice Brown parallel each other in that each was taught by her mother to please men even at the cost of self-respect. Perhaps Susan Nipper's lively disrespect for all about her keeps Florence balanced. These two share a remarkable bravery, but in her own way Alice Brown is brave too. She faces her own anger, expresses it, and then relents. It takes great courage for her to turn to Harriet Carker, whom she has insulted, and to ask her for help. It also takes courage for Harriet to respond with loyal friendship. Unlike the men in the story, the women cross the barriers of social class almost by ignoring them. The one man who can genially and gently accept social fall is Cousin Feenix, whose kindly loyalty to Edith makes his support acceptable to her, when she feels she can face no one. Dickens tries to do women justice in this book, showing that the pressure on them is fierce, but can be overcome by love.

The landscape of the book must be taken as a whole; overall this is a novel about London, despite the visits to Brighton; part of the wonder of the book is its ability to convey the number of different places of which London seems to be made up: the streets of small shops, grand houses, or places of finance, a harbour and port, quiet suburbs, and ramshackle tenements. The sense of a living city gives the book an underlying unity. Readers are left feeling that, although many stories have been told, many more also still going on. That is a major achievement for any writer—to leave his readers hoping that he will write more.

Part 4

Hints for study

Points for detailed study

1. The plot of *Dombey and Son* is complicated and has several sub-plots. Give attention to the way in which these are fitted together to make one novel. Examine the manner in which characters meet other characters. In this book such meetings seldom occur just by coincidence. Dickens wrote the novel in a series of thirty-two page pamphlets: consider how this form of publication may have fitted in with his using plots with sub-plots, perhaps by giving the reader more variety of characters to respond to, and by adding to the suspense in the novel.

2. This is a psychological novel. Consider the depth in Dickens's portrayal of the different characters. Although most change little, and only gradually, the reader comes to know them much better as the book goes on. When a character does something unexpected, as when Florence leaves home and goes to live at The Wooden Midshipman, or when Susan Nipper marries Mr Toots, consider how this development was prepared for in the previous portrayal of the character. Rob the Grinder, for instance, is one of the few bad children in Dickens's work. How does he become what he is; can he escape from a life of petty crime?

3. Study the *motifs* or central images of the story. These Notes consider the journey as one of the central ones. Even as the book closes, Florence and Walter have been on a long journey but return home and reconciled with Florence's father. Dickens himself was an inveterate traveller; as a writer he seems to have needed the stimulus that visiting new places gave him. Consider whether the many journeys are undertaken out of a common compulsive need, or whether some journeys are undertaken out of loyalty and duty. Other motifs are shipping and the sea. Think about what they mean to each character. Perhaps contrast them with the newer railways.

4. Think about the different women in the story. Some lead lives that are fulfilled; others are perverted or frustrated. How well does Dickens understand women? Is the difference between men and women wider than that between servants and those who employ them. Would his expectations for women seem fulfilling to most women today? Was housekeeping so much more complex then that it required more

intelligence and energy than now? Dickens makes most characters bad or good, but in *Dombey and Son* Edith Dombey and Alice Brown feel a mixture of good and bad impulses. How well does Dickens explain their emotions?

3. Dombey thinks of the moral traits as most important when he shows how people lead their lives. Show how this works out in individual characters' destinies. Think about how Florence grows up, and how the different situations in which she finds herself affect her. Pay special attention to Susan and her influence on Florence, and to the troubled relationship between Florence and Edith Dombey. Think about how taking responsibility changes a character. Contrast the two Carker brothers, one striving to repent and atone, the other resentfully preying on his employer.

6. How do the comic parts of this novel blend in with the rest? Does the overall seriousness of the book give a poignancy to the comedy? Does the feeling for minor characters make comedy about them seem less serious, and make the main characters seem perhaps at times eccentric? Dickens comedy is of a very special kind and the more you study it the more complex and rewarding you will find it. It depends on exaggeration and incongruity, but with a centre of recognisable truth.

Specimen questions and answers

Read each question carefully when you are attempting an answer. Remember to *answer* the question and not just to write what you know about Dickens. Develop a few main points in your argument and if you have time try to think of answers to possible questions arising from them or to reply to objections. Write as clearly and fluently as you can, remembering that your answer is itself an essay. Whenever you can, refer directly to the book you are studying, citing examples to illustrate your meaning.

Here are a few sample questions and answers to them given in outline form.

A. What social comment is made by Dickens in *Dombey and Son*?

To answer this question you need to have a thorough knowledge of the text. Impersonal, capitalist values are criticised. This is one of the *themes* of the book. Dombey does not really know his employees. He takes no personal responsiblity for them. While he dreams of the great future of the House of Dombey, Carker handles the day-to-day decisions. Carker can be malicious, as well as thoughtless. He regards Walter's fate as of little concern to him when he sends him to

Barbados. He treats his brother John Carker with resentment, and he does not help him to rise again in the firm. Dickens is making the point that there is no way for a business to be completely impersonal and just. Dombey's servants at home also suffer from his deliberate unconcern, epitomised by his insistence that Polly Toodle neither visit her family nor keep her own name. Dombey's trading establishment is set in deliberate contrast to the old-fashioned shop, The Wooden Midshipman, where business may not go well, but is done in a proper spirit; goods are sold there that are of real value to people who need them. The uncertainty of Dombey's finances is part of the cruelty of the new system.

Dickens, however, shows himself to be more ambivalent about the railways which had altered the British way of life as they spread across the country in the 1840s and 1850s. The railways bring prosperity to some of the poor, although they tend to destroy local enterprise. Through them great power is released that both benefits and menaces people. Dickens talks about the railways as inhuman energy which people cannot fully grasp.

Dickens also comments on the role of women and draws parallels between the destinies of Alice Brown and Edith Dombey as they sell themselves, Alice unwittingly, Edith knowingly. But through a minor character, Miss Tox, Dickens shows that this fate is not inevitable. Florence faces up to Walter's possible death and a possible life of spinsterhood bravely. This bravery is richly rewarded. The differences of character are shown to be more important in people's lives than differences in social class.

Dickens satirises the new education which crams facts into students's heads. This is a theme to which he often returns in other books. The teachers are misguided but not unkind. But much unhappiness is generated by the bad teaching system, which is of little profit to anyone.

The social panorama is always present in Dickens's imagination and so *Dombey and Son* portrays London as a city of great contrasts, with wealthy squares and extensive slums.

B. 'The joys of the spirit are found by characters who are denied the joys of the world.' Comment.

This is a thematic question that asks you to think about why the author makes the action of the story proceed in certain ways. You can reply by developing certain parts of the plot showing how characters are affected. For example, Florence loses her wealth, first voluntarily by leaving home, and later her potential wealth is lost when Dombey's fortune fails. Florence, however, enters fully into a life rich in companionship by going to live at The Wooden Midshipman, and finds first independence and later freedom to love Walter without any regrets or worldly anxieties. Walter loses hope of advancement in Dombey's firm, but gains the freedom to ask Florence to marry him and share in a life of adventure.

Because the theme is so prevailing in the book, it affects minor characters as well as major. For example, Miss Tox loses the companionship of Mrs Chick, but gains the more genuine friendship of the Toodles. Mr Toots finds no joy in his money but gains the guiding light of Susan Nipper to help him in his life.

You could balance this with Harriet and John Carker giving some of their income anonymously to Mr Dombey after his fall; as they have lived frugally for so long they feel no need of extra money, and know that Dombey cannot change his habits completely. The Toodles' rise can also be discussed—Dickens shows, fairmindedly, that relatively poor people benefit from more money if they are able to stay friendly with their old circle. You could make the fine distinction that Dickens is not against money, is not taking an ascetic view, but is saying that the lack of money can only cause a dreary struggle to burden people's lives; it cannot destroy their spirit.

C. Mothers and daughters play a big part in *Dombey and Son*. Discuss Mrs Skewton and Edith, Mrs Brown and Alice, and finally the shadowy mother and foster mothers of Florence.

Mothers are both good and bad in *Dombey and Son*. They pass on the kind of life that they themselves lead. You could begin by discussing Mrs Skewton and Edith, and the parallel characters of Mrs Brown and Alice, showing how Mrs Brown feels some rough fondness for her 'fine gel' and can be roused to angry passion over Carker's wronging of her, whereas Mrs Skewton continues a life of flirtation into old age. Her feeling for her daughter consists of helping her to acquire 'accomplishments' such as piano-playing and drawing, that will make her more attractive. Both women, however, expect their daughters to attract and allure men and give them little dignity in their own right. Because of the rich plot structure of the book you will be able to show how Edith sometimes overcomes these influences and mothers Florence more genuinely, trying to care for her welfare and peace of mind.

The shadowy figure of Florence's own mother is a benign influence of memory. But Susan Nipper, despite her youth, is an actual mother, plain-speaking and strict. She is a good guide for Florence.

D. What view does Dickens take of education in *Dombey and Son*?

This is a straightforward question which you can answer from the text, although any knowledge you have of the education of the period will be useful. You can begin with the schooling of Paul and Florence at home. There they learn a little. Then they go to Mrs Pipchin's in Brighton. They learn a little there, but Dickens suggests that their real education comes from their observation of other people. Dr Blimper's Academy is a place of facts, facts, and more facts, where misguided attempts are made to prepare young people for life by stuffing their heads with knowledge. Dickens suggests that this is harmless except that it leaves the young people little room for the knowledge they really need. Walter Gay, on the other hand, serves a kind of apprenticeship in Sol's shop, but goes on to serve as a junior clerk in Dombey's firm. This, too, is a kind of apprenticeship to a particular form of work. Later he will learn sailor's work in the same way. This practical education is a great contrast to that offered to most middle-class girls, who learn 'accomplishments' such as piano-playing and drawing. These skills are meant to help them to find husbands mainly by signalling their diligence and social status. This habit is shown at its most innocent in the case of Miss Tox. Little or no education, however, comes the way of Alice Brown; like many of the poor she falls outside the educational systems, private, public, or religious. Working-class girls who learn a trade are lucky. They can support themselves. One of the relatively new experiments, the Charitable Grinders' School, to which Mr Dombey sends Rob Toodle, is summed up as brutal. You might consider whether any of these methods of education is described with comic exaggeration or melodramatic excess, and discuss where people find their real education, the education of the heart that they learn from their families and friends.

E. 'The message of the book is, overall, compassion.' Comment.

This is a very open question giving you a chance to write about good and bad characters. It allows you to describe the action of the story and reveal its themes. You might consider whether or not the book is, overall, optimistic and positive. The question allows you to discuss Dickens's values.

Part 5

Suggestions for further reading

The text

A full edition of Dickens's works currently in print is *The New Oxford Illustrated Dickens*, Oxford University Press, London, 1948–. A good paperback edition of *Dombey and Son* is the Signet Classic edition, based on the 'Charles Dickens' edition of 1867, which Dickens revised for the press.

Critical works

CHESTERTON, G.K., *Charles Dickens*, Methuen, London, 1906. A famous early critical study by a lively essayist and fellow novelist.

FORSTER, JOHN, *The Life of Charles Dickens*, Chapman and Hall, London, 1872–4. The authorised life by Dickens's oldest friend.

HOUSE, HUMPHRY, *The Dickens World*, Oxford University Press, London, 1941. A historical study of Dicken in his period.

JOHNSON, E., *Charles Dickens: His Tragedy and Triumph*, rev. and abridged, Allen Lane, London, 1977. This is probably the definitive biography.

LEAVIS, F.R. AND LEAVIS, Q.D., *Dickens the Novelist*, Pelican Books, Harmondsworth, 1970. This includes a long essay on *Dombey and Son*.

MILLER, J. HILLIS, *Charles Dickens: The World of His Novels*, Indiana University Press, Bloomington, 1969. This is an attempt to portray Dickens's 'imaginative universe', through scrutiny of his style and recurrent images.

WILSON, ANGUS, *The World of Charles Dickens*, Penguin Books, London, 1972. A full and lively account of Dickens's career, with interesting critical remarks, by a fellow novelist.

Background

BEST, GEOFFREY, *Mid-Victorian Britain*, Weidenfeld & Nicolson, London, 1971. A good general book about the period.

The author of these notes

SUZANNE BROWN completed her BA in English 'with honour and distinction' at Mount Holyoke College in Massachusetts. She has a diploma in Anglo-Irish literature and a PH D degree from Trinity College, Dublin, and also holds a higher diploma in Education. She has worked as a lecturer and tutor at Trinity College, Dublin, and is the author of York Notes on Hawthorne's *The Scarlet Letter* and Dickens's *Oliver Twist*. She has also published poetry, and essays dealing with educational topics.